GOOD·OLD·DAYS®

HOLIDAY FUN
in the
GOOD OLD DAYS™

Edited by Ken and Janice Tate

Holiday Fun in the Good Old Days™

Editors: Ken and Janice Tate

Managing Editor: Barb Sprunger

Editorial Assistant: Sara Meyer

Copy Supervisor: Michelle Beck

Copy Editors: Mary O'Donnell, Läna Schurb

Publishing Services Director: Brenda Gallmeyer

Art Director: Brad Snow

Assistant Art Director: Nick Pierce

Graphic Arts Supervisor: Ronda Bechinski

Production Artists: Nicole Gage, Janice Tate

Production Assistants: Marj Morgan, Judy Neuenschwander, Jessica Tate

Photography Supervisor: Tammy Christian

Photography: Matt Owen

Photo Stylist: Tammy Steiner

Printed in China

First Printing: 2009

Library of Congress Number: 2007937752

ISBN: 978-1-59217-214-6

Good Old Days Customer Service: (800) 829-5865

We would like to thank the following for the art prints used in this book.
For fine-art prints and more information on the artists featured in *Holiday Fun in the Good Old Days* contact:
Curtis Publishing, Indianapolis, IN 46202, (317) 633-2070, All rights reserved, www.curtispublishing.com
Jim Daly, P.O. Box 25146, Eugene, OR 97402, www.jimdalyart.com

1 2 3 4 5 6 7 8 9

Dear Friends of the Good Old Days,

Holidays back when I was a young snip of a boy were like a road map to the year.

Yes, the pathway of each annual cycle was filled with long stretches of hard work, whether you are talking about the chores around the house and farm, or the seemingly never-ending school year.

© Jim Daly

But along that winding road that was life in the Good Old Days were those wonderful roadside parks called holidays that refreshed the weary traveler and readied him or her for the next few miles of the journey.

Each season invigorated us. The stops along the annual highway were like scenic views, making us slow down long enough to realize the precious passage of time. They forced us to take the time to enjoy our fellow travelers, be they family, neighbors or just pilgrims with whom we momentarily crossed paths.

It was the idea of that road map that led my dear wife Janice and me to pull together the stories for this special book of memories. The pages of *Good Old Days* magazine have always been well-seasoned with the special holiday memories of our readers. We decided it was time to

take that spice of life and produce a book that would bring back the wide-eyed wonder of all the holiday points of interest along the highway of life.

In the pages of this book you will find memories of the spiritual and innocent, the patriotic and political, the romantic and familial calendar dates that we awaited almost breathlessly. "Are we there yet?" was always the question at the forefront of our minds. These stories will remind you that the weeks leading up to them were like highway signs:

Easter—2 weeks
Mother's Day—2 months
Independence Day—12 weeks
Christmas—9 months

Spring brought with its annual visit the profound joy of Easter and its promise of regeneration, both spiritual and physical. But there was also the fun that revolved around April Fools' Day, May Day and Mother's Day.

Summer brought Memorial Day, Father's Day, the patriotic Flag and Independence Days, and at the end of the season, Labor Day. Autumn had, of course, Halloween, but also Veteran's Day and Thanksgiving.

Winter capped the annual cycle of holidays like a snow-capped mountain vista. Christmas, New Year's and Valentine's Day all brightened up the dreariness of winter and prepared us for the start of the springtime trip through the holidays again.

Janice and I hope this package of holiday memories reminds you of the days when our whole world stopped for holidays. Today we speed on past them like we are on an interstate highway, but take the exit marked, "Memory Lane" and join us for a leisurely visit to Holiday Fun in the Good Old Days.

❧ Contents ❧

Joyous Springtime • 6

Papaw and the Egg Hunt......................................8
Easter Season 12
The Chocolate Easter Tree 14
Easter as a Child 16
The Easter Bouquet..18
Easter Bonnets 19
The Magic Rabbit 20
Winner by a Hare 21
A Pennsylvania Dutch Easter 22
April School Day 24
The Prank That Wasn't a Prank 26
April Fool 27
Dance Around the Maypole 28
Remembering 29
May Day! May Day!..30
May Day..32
The Day Teacher Kissed Me 33
May Baskets 34
A Beautiful Ritual..35
Mama's Diamond Ring.......................................36
Mother's Day Carnations 38
A Lapful of Flowers...40
Mother's Rosebuds...41
M-O-T-H-E-R 43
Dinner on the Grounds.......................................44

Glorious Days of Summer • 46

Decoration Day 48
In Flanders Fields..50
Yesteryear Memorial Day 51
Fruit Jars and Lilacs...52
My Father's Hands...53
Family Tradition...54
Memorial Day Snow of 1947 56
Hometown Parades 58
Good Old Memorial Days 60
That's My Daddy 62
A Rose for Father's Day 64
Laurels for Father..65
Fly the Flag High!..66
Stars and Stripes Forever 68
The Fourth in the '40s..70
The Night John Whistled at Grandma 72
A Big Boom 74
A Boy, a Dog and a Race 75
July Fourth, 1935 76

The Cannon 79
My Skyrocket Ride 80
My Most Memorable Fourth of July 82
Knights of Labor Holiday 84
An Important Day 85

Autumn Treats • 86

All Hallow's E'en 88
Halloween Fun 91
A Very Expressive Jack-o'-Lantern 92
The Outhouse 96
It Was a Scream 97
The Halloween Prank That Backfired 98
Ef You Don't Watch Out! 99
The Trickster Tricker 100
Not for the Faint of Heart 102
A Halloween Ride 103
Scared Stiff 104
The Stranger 105
An Unforgettable Date 106
Armistice Day 109
When Masqueraders Reigned 112
An Unforgettable Thanksgiving 114
Over the River, Through the Wood 116
A Boy's Thanksgiving Day 118
Anything for Thanksgiving? 119
Thanksgiving 1935 120

Celebrations of Winter • 122

A Homemade Christmas 124
Chocolate-Covered Cherries 127
The Little Red Rocking Chair 128
Exactly as It Was Meant to Be 129
Now Is the Time for Christmas 130
Christmas Also Meant Fireworks 134
Measles at Christmas, 1935 136
A Visit From St. Nicholas 139
Flexible Flyer 140
The Night Santa Dropped In 142
A Basket Full of Christmas 144
Grandma's Lasting Gift 146
Christmas Bells 147
Holiday Remembrance 148
A Howling Success 150
A New Year's Celebration 151
Happy New Year! 152
Rose Parade 1949 154
The Best Valentine 155
A Valentine From Dad 156
Old-Time Valentine Pattern 159
Little Chocolate Heart 160

HOWARD SCOTT

Joyous Springtime

Chapter One

For a young boy on the farm back in the Good Old Days, there was no greater time on earth than joyous springtime.

I couldn't wait until the first jonquils of the season pushed their way into view—oftentimes fighting their way through late snow blanketing the Ozark Mountains that were my home.

Jonquils were the early blooming harbingers of joyous springtime, soon to be followed by peach and apple blossoms. The perfume of our fruit trees drifted across our yard and into my brain, bringing with it the promise of carefree, barefoot days ahead.

We always called our yellow jonquils "Easter lillies," even though they really weren't. But their appearance did mean Easter was just around the corner, and Easter meant egg hunts and Easter bunnies and special chicken dinners after church.

When I was a youngster, Easter in our family always began with an egg-coloring party on Saturday night. Mama had purchased a package of PAAS egg coloring on her last visit to the general store in town. After hard-boiling a dozen eggs (four each for her three youngsters), she set four bowls out for dying the eggs red, blue, green or yellow.

We put our eggs in whatever color we wished, rolling the egg in the dye or using a spoon to ladle the color over the egg.

I remember asking Mama if I could move my partially blue egg into the green bowl to see what the result might be. She said that the blue dye would contaminate the green color, so my budding artistic hopes were dashed.

Jonquils were the early blooming harbringers of joyous springtime.

(In later years, when times were a bit better, I remember getting four watercolor brushes for the dye bowls and being allowed to paint swashes and swirls—maybe even a bunny face—on my eggs.)

I know most families had an Easter Bunny equivalent of Santa Claus, but we didn't. Mama and Daddy talked a bit about the Easter Bunny, but there were no midnight visits carrying with them the mystery and excitement of Christmas.

I don't know if the Easter Bunny tradition was just too financially burdensome on a family budget already stretched to the breaking point, or if it was just harder to sell the story to youngsters. But for whatever reason, the whole bunny myth never caught on in the Tate household.

Mama and Daddy did hide our eggs the next morning so we could have our own Easter egg hunt, and there was a much more expansive one after church later in the day. The church Easter egg hunt meant meeting up with my best friends, sharing the thrill of the hunt and then the shared candy treats provided by parents for special prizes.

But church also had its sobering side as well. The story of the Messiah who gave His life for the sins of the world, but who conquered death through the resurrection was one that would stay with me throughout my life.

Easter was just the beginning of holiday fun back in the Good Old Days. Soon to follow were April Fools' Day, May Day and all the rest. Yes, joyous springtime was bursting out all around us. What more could a farm boy ask for?

—Ken Tate

Papaw and The Egg Hunt

By Cynthia Hudson

When I hear someone fondly call his grandfather "Papaw," memories of my own dear Papaw flood my heart and mind. My maternal grandparents were Tom and Minta Parkes. We lived in northern middle Tennessee in the small community of Winklers in Macon County. My grandparents were part of the Winklers and Bethany communities from the 1920s through the 1970s.

Papaw Parkes was a farmer and a church-going man who loved to have a little fun along his way in life. One of his favorite church-going seasons was spring, with the annual Easter Sunday egg hunt at our little country church.

Back in the early 1950s, many large families were part of our country church. One family I recall had 14 children, and two other families had 12 children each. There were many smaller families besides. We all attended Sunday school at Bethany Missionary Baptist Church. With so many children, we had a big egg hunt on Easter Sunday!

Everyone in the community looked forward to Easter. Children got new Sunday clothes. Mothers and grandmothers spent the weeks before Easter getting new Sunday clothes ready for the big event.

Gram Parkes always saved money from selling eggs to help dress my cousin and me in matching Easter clothes. Gram ordered fancy little dresses, coats, hats and other cute but itchy outfits from the Montgomery Ward or Sears, Roebuck catalogs.

Other mothers and grandmothers did the same in their own way to be sure that their children came to Sunday school dressed in their newest Sunday best. A lot of well-dressed boys and girls happily headed to the egg hunt each Easter Sunday.

Papaw Parkes loved Easter. He had attended school only long enough to learn the basics, and so he did not read well enough to enjoy the Bible-reading classes of

© *The Egg Hunter* by Jim Daly

Sunday school. But at events like the egg hunt, he could do things he was really good at doing. Papaw loved the egg hunt. He got to hide eggs and try to make the prize egg especially difficult to find. Sometimes he even dug holes in the ground and covered them with leftover fall leaves.

The eggs to be hidden were boiled, decorated hen eggs. Candy eggs were scarce in those days, but hen eggs were plentiful—and traditional. Eggs were almost always fresh because we had gathered them the day before.

It was also traditional to prepare the eggs on Sunday morning, just before going to the egg hunt. The eggs had to be cooked, cooled and dipped in food coloring mixed with vinegar water. Sometimes we even had an egg-coloring kit with little color tablets that dissolved in vinegar. The kits had a small copper-wire holder that we used to dip the eggs into the colored vinegar water. We also had boiled eggs for breakfast on Easter Sunday because it was almost impossible to boil eggs without cracking a few in the process. Preparing the eggs for our egg hunt was a labor of love and tradition.

One year my parents and I had the honor of bringing the prize egg to the hunt. That year, we had a strawberry patch that needed weeding and debugging, and we used a flock of geese for the chore. If we were very diligent, we could find the nests of the geese and gather their eggs. To my astonishment, I even found a goose egg in a small pool in our barnyard stream. We were often surprised by where we found the goose eggs.

Just in time for Easter, we found a good goose egg that we could use for the prize. A big egg made the prize more realistic. Mama had saved enough aluminum foil to wrap the egg so that it appeared to be silver. It made a real shiny prize egg that would be easy to distinguish from the hen eggs we hunted to try to win the prize for finding the most eggs.

Papaw Parkes was well prepared for each egg hunt. He would arrive at church with a big smile and a salt shaker. He was always ready to eat any cracked egg that might not be fit to hide. He also sometimes carried a stick for digging a hole to hide the prize egg. He thought the prize egg should present a challenge; it

should be earned by hard work. It should not be an easy find!

As my grandparents entered the church, you could hear Gram saying to Papaw, "Now Tom, please don't hid the prize egg in the dirt again.

Tom B. and Minta Parkes holding the author.

You know that the mothers don't want their children to come back to the church with their clothes all ruined and muddy! The mothers will be mad at you!"

Papaw would reply with a grin and a twinkle in his eye, "Aw, Minnie, it wouldn't be any fun if the prize egg is too easy to find! We've got to have a little fun!" Gram would shake her head and smile. *You will never learn!* she would think to herself.

Papaw would laugh, and I'm almost sure he

thought, *I'll find a good* deep *hole this year for the prize egg.*

Sunday school began at 10 a.m. on Easter Sunday morning. Children, parents—everyone—was dressed in new clothes. My Great-Grandmother Davis, Gram's mother, taught the smallest children in what we called the Card Class. Great-Grandma would hand out a greeting-card–size lesson to each child.

Left to right: E.G. Williams, Tom Parkes (the author's grandfather), Ellis Davis (the author's step-great-grandfather), Aubrey Prowell, Dave Lanford and Lucian Ferguson in the back.

Each card had a Bible picture on the front, the matching Bible story inside, and simple questions to answer on the back. On Easter we would traditionally have the resurrection story. While we had our lesson, the gentlemen of the church were busy hiding the eggs outside on the church grounds.

At the appointed signal, the Sunday school classes would be called to the church doors. Young children would line up first, and the junior class (children ages 10 and up) would be next in line. Teenagers and adults stood back to watch the fun and mayhem begin.

On one particular Easter Sunday, Papaw was in his best form. He had managed to hide the prize egg so well that no one had been able to find it! The regular Easter eggs were all accounted for, but the prize egg still was safely hidden. Papaw led a group of eager little boys in clean, new Sunday clothes to a clump of rotting tree stumps. "The prize egg is somewhere around these tree stumps," Papaw said.

The boys dug with newfound enthusiasm. Rotting leaves, fresh muddy mulch and pure mud began to fly. Luckily for the moms, most of the girls were not anxious to dig through the mud, but the boys sure didn't let a little muck deter them.

The men's laughter could be heard for miles around, but the moms and grandmothers were thinking ahead to the messy results—and not many of them were laughing!

Finally, a shout of, "I've found it!" rang out, and one young fellow emerged from the mud, proudly holding up the foil-covered goose egg.

The boy was covered with mud and rotting leaves, and smudges streaked his smiling face. Papaw had done another good job of hiding the prize egg. And everyone had fun—well, *almost* everyone!

As they left the church, the women could be overhead talking about it. "I sure wish Mr. Tom wouldn't hide those prize eggs in the dirt!" one said.

"Do you think Mr. Tom would like to wash those new clothes sometime this week?"

I could see Gram cringe and shake her head at Papaw with that "I told you so" look. But Papaw would simply smile, wink and shake a little salt on his fresh-boiled egg.

No doubt about it; Papaw had enjoyed his kind of egg hunt back in those simple Good Old Days. ❖

Easter Season

By Barbara Potts

We grew up in beautiful East Texas. Daddy had hired on with the Atlantic Oil Co. at the peak of the Depression in 1934. We moved from White Oak, Texas, into the Carlisle school district near Joinerville. We lived in a company house located on Daddy's work lease, the Strickland "B." Our neighbors were Mr. and Mrs. Slentz and their three boys. Their house was down the oil road about one fourth of a mile to the south of us.

Spring was always a welcome time. Tiny wildflowers would begin to show as the weeds began to wake. The hickory, sweet gum, elm and oak trees would put on their new leaves in many shades of green, and there would be a sprinkling of dogwood blossoms.

Mother would take us kids—Margaret, Barbara, Bobbie and Bud—shopping for new Easter shoes. We would wear our new, serviceable shoes to church on Easter Sunday, on Sundays through the summer, and then into the next school year.

Our mother was a wonderful seamstress, as was our Aunt Oderra. They would make new dresses for the girls. Sometimes Mother would sew Bud's shirt and a dress for herself. Other times she would buy them.

On Easter Sunday at Carlisle Baptist Church, everyone was happy and well-dressed. We looked beautiful in our spring clothes, especially the ladies in their new spring hats. Everyone had come to worship, and of course, to sing *Crown Him With Many Crowns.*

Of great interest to us was the kids' part of Easter. It really got under way on Saturday night, after the supper dishes were washed and dried. Then it was time to prepare for the grand egg hunt!

Mother had boiled two dozen or more eggs, some from our own chicken yard, and they were placed in the center of the table. Then five or six cups—the old ones with the cracks—were put out. Into each was placed a little vinegar and a powdered dye: pale yellow, pink, blue, green, purple and sometimes orange. The dye packets also came with little tissue-paper transfers of rabbits, chicks and flowers, and wire dipping holders. Hot water was carefully poured into each cup. After the dye was stirred, we were ready to create Easter eggs.

This photo was taken on Easter Sunday, 1937, by the author's mother. The pine grove where the eggs were hidden is visible in the background. The children at the left and third, fifth and sixth from the left are from the author's family. The older boys wouldn't have missed the fun, but apparently wouldn't be caught with an Easter basket! The girls had already changed from their new Easter finery into play clothes.

The little transfer designs had been individually cut, and oh, how I hoped someone wouldn't take the one I really wanted before it was my turn to choose! We also used our crayons to draw designs on the eggs. The dye would not "take" over the crayon drawing.

If Daddy was working a night shift, we would always wait until he made his rounds and had time to stop by the house to join us.

Finally it was Sunday after church. Aunt Oderra and Uncle Jess Hunter would drive from New London after their church service to our house for Easter dinner and the egg hunt. They owned Hunter's Drugstore, and they always brought candy eggs, chicks and rabbits to add to the hunt. I often wondered if these were treats they had set aside for us, or if they simply hadn't sold, but either way, they certainly enriched the day, and we loved having our aunt and uncle with us.

Neighbor children knew who conducted the best hunt. The number of kids grew as they all brought their baskets and eggs.

The hunt was laid out by the men attending. It was always held in the beautiful pine grove just north of our home, across the road from the Strickland No. 3 oil well.

Mother and Aunt Oderra would stand guard over the kids inside the house with the shades drawn while the eggs and surprises were hidden. When the men gave the signal, the ladies would walk us down to the grove. Bursting with excitement, we would wait for the signal: "*Go!*"

Someone always found the one-of-a-kind prize egg. The lucky one was rewarded with a pack of gum or a candy bar.

It was a wonderful day, and we all knew that we had had a very happy Easter. We also knew that we would probably have egg-salad sandwiches in our lunch sacks the next day. ❖

The Chocolate Easter Tree

By Joyce Normandin

*M*y friends and I were experts on candy. We each had a sweet tooth that was always ready and willing to chomp on something yummy. We made many trips with our pennies to the candy store on Union Street and Sixth Avenue in Brooklyn and spent a lot of time picking out the best deals, noses pressed against the glass display case.

Kits candy was a great bargain. In the 1940s we could buy them for a penny, and there were eight or 10 in a pack. There were also sugar candy dots on paper, and you got lots of dots. If you had 5 cents, you might buy NECCO wafers. This meant that if you or a friend were lucky and had a few pennies, there would be some to share.

These girls are enjoying the contents of their Easter baskets.

One of our favorite times was Halloween. It was like the candy-greed olympics. Christmas was nice because our family received gift boxes of choco-lates, which were a better quality than penny candy. Candy canes hung from the Christmas tree, and we also enjoyed hard ribbon candy, for which my dentist was forever grateful.

But we all agreed that Easter was the best. We got some volume, but quality, too, as evidenced by those luscious chocolate bunnies. My friend, Dorrie, always got the best Easter chocolates. We could not compete with her. She had a very rich uncle who would send her the biggest chocolate bunny.

After church, dressed in our Easter finery, we all gathered on someone's steps with our Easter baskets and compared. I usually got yellow marshmallow chicks, lots of jelly beans, some chocolate eggs, a candy egg with a hole in the side for viewing the Easter scene with-in, and a nice chocolate bunny with a pink ribbon around its neck. The rest of my friends received about the same thing.

One Easter, however, was a little different. Dorrie did not have a basket to show. We tried to figure this out. We had noticed that a delivery truck had stopped in front of her apartment building the day before Easter and delivered a huge white box. We were sure that it must have contained either a big doll or a large stuffed bunny. We felt a little sorry for her because she had no candy, but we wanted to know about the box and see the doll or stuffed bunny. So, we begged and nagged until she finally invited us inside to reveal the mystery.

We all trooped into her bedroom, clutching our baskets, and our eyeballs popped in amazement. Sitting on a table was the hugest, most humongous chocolate confection we had ever laid eyes on. We were dumbstruck.

It was about 2 feet tall and shaped like a tree stump. Sawed-off limbs were scattered around the trunk, and on each limb perched a lovely bird made of candy. At the bottom were three tiny white-chocolate bunnies sitting on coconut that was dyed green, like grass, with pastel candy flowers strewn about. Some candy butterflies seemed to be fluttering about the tree stump. It was stupendous, gorgeous, colossal—a veritable memorial to the Easter chocolate frenzy. We were all pea-green with envy.

After the initial shock, we all delved into our baskets and began to munch. All except Dorrie, that is. We looked at her, perplexed.

"Aren't you going to eat some of your chocolate tree?" we asked. Each of us imagined plunging into that chocolate fantasy. I myself had staked out one of those little candy birds.

"Nope," Dorrie replied. "It's just too pretty to eat, so I am going to save it just like it is."

This was unheard of. Whoever saved their Easter candy forever? We begged, but Dorrie was adamant. This masterpiece, this Mona Lisa of chocolate, would never be eaten.

We were horrified. Then we began to feel a little sorry for Dorrie, and I offered her a bite of my chocolate bunny. She bit off the ears, which was not a socially acceptable thing to do. In fact, it was an offense of the greatest magnitude. The ears were always saved for the owner.

It was stupendous, gorgeous, colossal—a veritable memorial to the Easter chocolate frenzy.

The chocolate confection was enshrined in her room, a light cotton cover over it. When we visited, we unveiled it and drooled, living in the futile hope that this would be the time when Dorrie would share. Alas, it was all in vain.

As time went by, it began to get a little weathered from pulling that cloth off and putting it back on. She didn't have air-conditioning, and as the weather warmed up, it began to lean and droop a little too.

It developed some whitish stuff on some of its parts. It didn't look quite so appetizing anymore. Some of the butterflies dropped off, and the birds were hanging onto the limbs for dear life. Still, when summer came in full force, Dorrie did not relent.

Then someone had a brilliant idea. Take a picture of it! She got her father to take a color photo, which he had enlarged and Dorrie put in a frame on her night table, in a place of honor.

"Now," she said, "everyone can have a piece of chocolate."

We gazed at the dilapidated specimen before us. It didn't look quite as appealing as it had in April. Now it was almost August. The summer heat had not been kind to it. We took one last look at the dismal confection in front of us and we all chorused at the same time, "No thanks, Dorrie." We just were not that brave.

Now her mother would not let Dorrie eat it, either. It ended up in the trash bin, a moldy testament to an Easter extravaganza that was meant to be eaten and enjoyed.

Dorrie's uncle passed away in November, so she never again got a huge chocolate work of art for Easter. It took me a long time—a couple of days in kid time—to forgive Dorrie for biting the ears off my chocolate bunny.

In a few years, we outgrew Easter baskets. Strange as it may seem, I vividly recall Dorrie's chocolate tree, but I cannot remember the Easter outfit that my mom sewed for me that year.

And I confess that I would not mind, just once more, getting an Easter basket filled with jelly beans and a chocolate bunny with a pink ribbon, just like I did back in the Good Old Days. ❖

Kenneth Stuart

Easter as a Child

By Leota Kuykendall

As a farm child during the Depression, I learned to have fun without expensive store-bought goodies. Holidays such as Easter provided opportunities for fun. I learned to anticipate the coming of Easter and tried to prolong its pleasures. Our family was religious, and I knew Lent was before Easter. The Saturday before Easter was especially busy. We prepared our new outfits to wear to church and eagerly chattered about the egg hunt we had planned with cousins for Sunday afternoon.

First we made nests where the bunny "laid" his eggs. When I was little, I didn't see this as humorous. However, farm child that I was, I woke up one day and realized that chickens—not the Easter Bunny—lay eggs.

We children used empty half-gallon syrup cans to make nests. If the cans didn't have handles, we took Daddy's hammer and a nail to make holes for a homemade wire handle. My father knew when we created our own handles to make buckets—we didn't return his hammer to its proper place in the car shed. When he'd go hunting for his hammer, his scolding was a sure consequence.

We ate eggs for breakfast daily, but only on Easter were they boiled.

We put fresh green grass and flowers in the buckets. We used pinks and bridal wreath, which bloomed in our yard, plus any wildflowers we could find. We placed our bunny nests on the steps of the porch to await the bunny's visit.

Early on Easter morning, Mother awakened us children, reminding us to check our nests. We hurried outdoors. In our nests of flowers lay warm pullet eggs colored red, green, blue and yellow. My mother rose early, boiled the eggs and colored them.

It was a treat to eat the eggs for breakfast. We ate eggs for breakfast daily, but only on Easter morning were they boiled. My mother teased us, telling us the bunny laid warm eggs.

We dressed for church in our new Easter apparel. When one of my baby sisters was 8 months old, my mother struggled to keep her Easter bonnet in place. The baby didn't like the bonnet with the tie under her chin. Mother tied the ribbon over and over, reprimanding the baby to leave her bonnet on because it looked pretty. My mother had sewed the bonnet to match the baby's new dress out of colorful feed sacks.

One hat story concerned one of my cousins. The array of flowers on her wide-brimmed hats was garden variety. At our house, hats had very small brims sparsely decorated with flowers because my mother considered fancy, big-brimmed hats to be a little sinful. My father complained about big hats blocking vision in church. I secretly hoped someday to grow up and wear a pretty, big-brimmed hat like my cousin wore.

After Sunday services, my mother talked about every hat in church. Once, I recall my cousin had an especially pretty Easter hat. But my mother talked about my cousin's hat with a very stern voice; she recognized the old hat with a new batch of flowers. My mother helped my grandmother put new flowers on her old hat for Easter. I listened to their worried conversation as they decorated the hat, discussing how to disguise the old hat enough so no one would guess it was old. I got the impression that it was a bit disgraceful to wear an old hat for Easter.

We also had new shoes stuffed with cotton in the toes. Often my mother talked in worried tones about our shoes as she tried to anticipate how much our feet would grow during the summer. When we went barefoot, my mother said, out feet spread out quickly.

When our oversized shoes didn't feel comfortable on Easter, we children complained. By the end of the summer, the shoes cramped our toes, which ignited more tears.

We got no sympathy, as Mother made it clear we could not afford more than one pair of new shoes for the season. Thus I grew up with a special fondness for going barefoot.

The focus on appropriate dress was a big deal. I recall many a quarrel with our mother as we children asserted choices. I sometimes cried because she wouldn't allow me to have my dress

Vintage postcard, House of White Birches nostalgia archives

The Easter Bouquet

By Letha Fuller

Bluebells rang the message,
"This is Easter Day,
Come to service, little friends,
Dress in bright array."

Lilies beamed in cream and white,
Tulips came in red.
Jonquil wore a yellow dress
And hat upon her head.

Iris came in purple;
Narcissus, we are told,
Looked lovely in her frills of white
With her crown of gold.

Sweet little hyacinths
Appeared in lilac, pink and rose,
But jack-in-the-pulpit
Wore very somber clothes.

What a congregation!
A very sweet bouquet
Came to celebrate
That happy Easter Day.

made from the feed sacks I liked best. The catalog ignited further differences.

Sears and Wards catalogs always graced our house. My siblings and I combed the pages to select hats and shoes. As I grew older, I learned to observe not only the fashions but the price. Once I recall sacrificing the hat I really wanted because my mother was ordering from one catalog to save on freight cost. I didn't understand and grumbled about my sacrifice.

Throughout my childhood, I didn't give up my concerns about appropriate dress for Easter. I did begin to doubt the value of all the fuss. I discovered the joy of Easter when the sad, slow music of Lent changed to lively Easter music.

I learned to enjoy the Easter stories full of hope and life following the sad stories of Lent. As I grew older, these joys overshadowed the petty bickering at home.

Once the early morning egg fun and the Easter services were over, I looked forward to visiting my maternal grandparents, where I enjoyed an egg hunt with my cousins. Although we only found a few eggs, the fun of hunting eggs with my cousins was my chief pleasure. Sometimes we'd find special eggs—blown-out eggshells filled with jelly beans, wrapped in colorful tissue paper and tied with a bow.

One special hunt included a prize egg. My cousin understood the idea of a prize egg, and talked and talked about finding it. I wondered what all the hoopla was about. He ran, wildly looking for the prize egg, and yelled with pleasure when he found a great big goose egg painted gold—a contribution from one of the youthful new aunts in the family.

My siblings and I re-created the Easter fun by hiding our eggs over and over. Eventually the boiled eggs cracked and broke, and the unwrapped candy eggs got dirty. Sometimes, weeks after Easter, I'd find a lost candy egg in the weeds. The game of hiding the eggs over and over was more fun for me than eating the eggs.

As I matured, I noticed that pretty colored eggs, colorful fashions and lively music on Easter brought forth joyful expressions in persons of all ages. I liked this effect. The joy and life of Easter blotted out for a while the atmosphere of lacking and fear during the hard Depression days of my childhood. ❖

Easter Bonnets

By Helen Patton Gray

I rving Berlin gave the world *Easter Parade*, which has become the theme song for that special springtime Sunday for all the years to come. Back in the 1930s, the *Kansas City Star* featured a rotogravure section in its Sunday edition. Printed in mystical brown sepia, it featured multiple photos of interesting people and events. The Easter editions with photos of the New York Easter Parade on Fifth Avenue were widely read and appreciated.

Picture-perfect women wore extravagant chapeaus, high-fashion dresses and elbow-length gloves. Some had high-button shoes.

Men wore striped suits, derbies and spats, and carried canes like Fred Astaire. All were extremely coordinated and elegant!

In tune with this Easter tradition, my mother made sure I had a new outfit expressly designed for the day. She sewed my dress on her old Singer treadle machine. Then we went shopping in downtown Kansas City for a frilly bonnet and black patent-leather shoes.

Sometimes Mom managed a new hat or purse for herself, if the budget wasn't too tight that month. My two brothers were outfitted with new knickers, shirts and ties, which they irreverently removed and hung in the closet after church.

By 1960, I was the mother of three. Gone were the days of those sepia newspaper inserts and extravagant Easter apparel. However, we celebrated Easter with church, new outfits and a bountiful ham dinner.

While thumbing through our photo albums, I came across the photo of my daughter and me taken in our front yard in Green Bay, Wis., in 1960. The custom of new Easter bonnets had prevailed until then.

Today I seldom wear a hat, nor does she. It's just one more lost tradition of the Good Old Days of the 1930s. ❖

The Magic Rabbit

By Helen D. Lewis

One of the best lessons I ever learned back in the Good Old Days came about because of a bunny rabbit. It was Easter, April 17, 1938, and I was 4 years old. We had just moved to the country the week before. I thought I was in heaven, for spring had come early that year, bringing an abundance of blooming daffodils, flowering quince and bridal wreath.

I loved the little farm that my parents had bought. It didn't matter that the house wasn't much to look at, or that Mom papered the walls with newspapers so they'd at least be clean. Nor did I mind the bare floors that she scrubbed with a broom and bleach water. I loved that old house with the wisteria vine growing up the side. I never liked the new house that replaced it two years later nearly as well. Old houses seem to have a personality of their own.

Anyway, that year there wasn't enough money to buy me an Easter basket. Mom worried about me being disappointed because all I was getting for Easter was colored eggs.

On Easter morning when I got up, Mom told me to wait about going out to hunt my Easter goodies; there had been drizzle the night before, and she wanted the grass to dry before I went out. I was sitting in the kitchen, looking out through one of the little panes that formed the big window, when a rabbit came hopping through the yard and down past the grape arbor. I couldn't believe my eyes—the Easter Bunny! I yelled, "Mommy, Mommy, he's here! The Easter Bunny is here! See?"

There was no holding me back then. I ran out the door and went in the direction from which the bunny had come. As luck would have it, that was the area where most of my beautiful eggs were hidden. Mom, still fearing I would be disappointed, explained that the bunny had probably run out of baskets before he got this far out in the country. Who cared? I was on cloud nine! I was the only person I knew who had seen the real Easter Bunny.

Now, after 60 years, I still remember that day, for it was my best Easter ever. Maybe he wasn't the real Easter Bunny, but that little rabbit worked magic for me that day and in later years as well. Seeing that little bunny meant more to me than any expensive basket ever could.

In later years, when I would fret about not being able to buy an expensive gift for someone, I would remember that Easter and remind myself that it is not the price of the gift that is important, but the enjoyment that it brings. ❖

Easter Greeting

Vintage postcard, House of White Birches nostalgia archives

Winner by a Hare

By Doris Auger

A week before Easter, my sister, Edith, my friend Stinky and I sat in front-row seats at the Park Theater. ("Stinky" was a nickname my friend and I had tagged on each other ever since seeing a certain Three Stooges episode.) The country was just emerging from the Great Depression.

The motion-picture house in Denver was crowded that day, and after the usual main features, the lights came on. Standing on the stage was a young man dressed in a suit, and he was announcing a contest. And sitting to his right was the biggest, most beautiful chocolate bunny I had ever seen. It peered at me through brightly colored cellophane wrapping.

"I need some contestants to see who can win this chocolate bunny," the young man said. I instantly leaped to my feet.

"Oh no, not again!" groaned Edith and Stinky. "She is always entering those dumb contests!"

Quickly I was on the stage, joining a half-dozen other children in a line. Most were 6 or 7 years old, just like me. A small, foil-wrapped Easter egg was set on the floor in front of each of us. "Get down on your knees and place your hands behind your back," the emcee ordered. "Now, with your nose, push the egg across the stage. The first one here (he pointed to himself) wins the chocolate bunny."

He pulled a whistle from his pocket, and a loud shrill filled the air. We were off!

Photo copyright © 2008, www.stockxpert.com

That floor was hard, and my knees ached! I pushed the egg with my nose, but it was a slow, agonizing ordeal. I could feel others passing me.

Suddenly, the egg wasn't moving, so I lifted my head a little. There was no egg on the floor! Then realization hit—that darn egg was stuck firmly to my nose! The marshmallow filling had apparently oozed out through a small opening.

Edith and Stinky's voices kept prodding me on. "You better go faster!" But they couldn't see my predicament. With my head still level with the floor and the egg on my nose, I moved faster with the egg barely skimming the floor. Then I felt a set of knees at my head. Strong arms lifted me up, my arms still behind me. The egg was still stuck on my nose, and my back was to the audience.

I had never seen such a startled look on a face before! Then the bewildered emcee softly uttered, "Oh, gee … " as two innocent, saucer-size eyes stared at him helplessly.

"Oh, what the heck!" he groaned. Then he set me down, plucked the egg from my nose, turned me to face the audience and raised my arm in the air. "The winnah!" he announced.

Clapping and whistling filled the theater. Even Edith and Stinky cheered as he placed the big bunny in my arms, and I returned to my seat. Cuddling the precious package, I tried to decide which part I would eat first. *An ear? a foot? that adorable fluffy chocolate tail? I might even give a little bite of the body to Edith and Stinky.*

I gently hugged the bunny again. The crinkly sound of the wrapping was music to my ears. ❖

A Pennsylvania Dutch Easter

By Mary Lu Eugley

I was the youngest in our family, which included my mother and father, a much older sister and my grandmother, who was "Nana" to all of us. We liked being together—especially at Easter.

Special baking took place before Lent. *Fashnachts*, or doughnuts, were made on Shrove Tuesday to introduce the season, and from this same mashed-potato dough, my mother would make Dutch cakes, cinnamon rolls and streusel coffee cake. Mmm, they were good! Tantalizing smells greeted me when I came home from school.

The girls played hopscotch on the front pavement, and the boys kicked the can in the street. After supper it was warm enough for the children to play outside again. We bounced balls against the garage door and hid behind bushes until we were tagged or made it to home base. At any rate, we had a lot of fun until, one by one, we were called in to go to bed.

On Easter Sunday I would go around the back yard with a basket and find all the nests of purple, blue and green speckled eggs hidden by the Easter Bunny. Mother would smile at my enthusiasm and place the collection in the big crystal bowl on the sideboard. Every neighbor and friend who visited us that day swapped Easter eggs with us.

We all dressed in our new finery for church on Easter. Nana put a new bunch of flowers on her little black hat, and Mother proudly displayed the rose corsage on her dress. I skipped happily between them, my new patent-leather shoes squeaking with each step.

The church was filled with Easter lilies, daffodils, hyacinths and tulips, and the air was heavy with their pungent sweetness. The pipe organ filled the church with music, and the choir sang "Hosanna!" until the rafters shook.

After the service, we delivered an Easter lily to a family who lived on the outskirts of town. On the lawn, a maple tree covered with brightly colored Easter eggs seemed to wave a greeting as we drove up the drive.

A young woman opened the door, and balancing a plump baby on her hip, took the proffered Easter lily in her other hand. "Thanks so much! We couldn't get to church today, but we thought of you all."

"Did the Easter Bunny put eggs on your tree?" I asked.

"We don't know. This morning we looked out the window, and there it was!"

"Come along," my father said to me, and with a "Happy Easter," we hurried back to the car.

At home, Easter baskets filled with chocolate bunnies, yellow chicks and colored jelly beans were hidden all around the house. As soon as my cousins arrived for dinner, we started our Easter hunt, looking through the flower beds in the yard and even under the car in the garage.

Finders were keepers, but each visiting family left an Easter basket on the walnut buffet in the dining room for our family to enjoy. Appetites for dinner were spoiled, but Easter only came once a year, and our parents didn't seem to mind.

After a long, happy day, I carried my shaggy, one-eyed stuffed Easter Bunny to bed with me. He would disappear during the night, but I knew he would reappear next year, just as the tree of Easter eggs had. ❖

Facing page: *Easter Time* by S.B. West, © House of White Birches nostalgia archives

April School Day

By Dorothy Stanaitis

As I watch the caravan of buses and cars drop children off at our local elementary school, I marvel at how different it all is from the peril-filled trips I made to second grade at James Rhoades School in Philadelphia during the 1940s. Each morning I faced a series of terrifying obstacles, and it took all the courage I could muster to overcome them.

Fortified by a goodbye kiss from my mother, I would bravely set off on my block-and-a-half walk to school. I refused to worry her with my problems, so she never knew what I had to endure each day. Still, she would wait on the front porch until I reached the lamppost in the middle of the block, where I would turn and wave a final goodbye. Then she would go into our house, and I would face my morning trials.

The first challenge was the neighbor's dog, Brownie. He was tied to their front porch railing each morning, and he flew into a frenzy of leaping and barking as I scurried past. I worried that his chain would snap or the porch railing would break, unleashing the menacing, 12-pound ball of fury. My heart pounded as I raced by their house. And I had to do that racing so carefully, jumping and leaping down the sidewalk.

"Dorothy," she said, "the school called. They're having special classes today."

The neighbors smiled as they watched the little girl they thought was trying some fancy hopping and skipping. They couldn't know that my curious gait was devised to avoid damaged pavement. After all, every second-grader knew that if you stepped on a crack, you'd break your mother's back. And if you stepped on a line, you'd break your father's spine.

This hopping, skipping and dodging had to be speedy, too, because every second-grader also knew that if we were late for school, we would be sent to the forbidden corner of the school basement—the janitor's room. There we would be beaten with a cat-o'-nine-tails. We knew this because the sixth-graders had told us so.

When I reached the corner where I had to cross the street, my vigilance increased. We seldom saw traffic go by since most of our neighbors had put their cars away for the duration of World War II. Still, I carefully checked both ways two times before racing madly to the other side of the street.

Then I had just half a block to go to the safety of the school playground, which was surrounded by a 6-foot wrought-iron fence. Once inside that fence, the only problem I might have would be my classmates' teasing if I had lost one of the ribbons that tied the ends of my braids, inelegantly called "pigtails" on the playground.

But more than the teasing, I dreaded the look on my mother's face as she took a few coins from her little black change purse and sent me once again to Diamond's Dry Goods to buy a replacement ribbon. Mrs. Diamond knew me by name from my frequent visits.

How I looked forward to Saturdays, when I could take a break from those weekday terrors. Relieved of the fear of crippling my parents by a careless misstep, I helped my mother dust the living room as we listened to one of our favorite radio programs, *Grand Central Station, Crossroads of a Million Private Lives.* In the afternoon, I could go roller-skating with my friends or join the crowd at the Frolic or Belmont movie theater for the matinee. Saturdays were always stress-free and fun.

But one Saturday morning, my mother came into my bedroom and shook me awake, gently but urgently. "Dorothy," she said, "the school called. They're having special classes today."

I looked at the clock, flew out of bed, got ready and dashed out of the house. If I didn't speed to school, I would have to face the janitor's wrath for being late. I never hurried as quickly as I did that day.

Leaping and jumping over the sidewalk cracks, I ran past barking Brownie. When I reached the lamppost, I stopped for the usual good-bye wave to my mother. But instead of waving, my mother was beckoning to me, calling me back to her. What could she want? If I went back, I would surely be late for school. But how could I disobey my mother? I ran back home as quickly and carefully as I could.

Panting and out of breath, I ran up our porch steps. When I reached her, my mother hugged me and laughed. "April Fool!"

I stared at her. I couldn't believe my luck. I was spared! I wouldn't be late for school after all. I wouldn't be sent to the janitor. I was safe at home with my mother. It was just a joke, an April Fools' joke.

Later, I overheard my mother telling her friends about it. She kept saying how glad she was that I hadn't been angry. She said I was a good sport. I was willing to take credit for sportsmanship, but it had really been simple relief that made me laugh at her practical joke on that long-ago April Fools' morning. ❖

1931 *People's Popular Monthly,* House of White Birtches nostalgia archives

The Prank That Wasn't a Prank

By Audrey Corn

April Fools' Day was my least favorite holiday back in the 1940s, when I was growing up in Brooklyn, N.Y. I knew that sooner or later, somebody would trick me. That somebody was always my big cousin, Emmy.

One April Fools' Day, Emmy told me that she had "plans." "You and your sister, Jennie, better watch out!" Emmy warned.

How could I watch out? Emmy's family lived down the street from us, and Emmy spent half her life at my house, snooping through my belongings. Last April Fools' Day, Emmy had snuck into the bedroom that I shared with my sister. Emmy rummaged through our bureau drawers and tied all our underwear in tight little knots!

Cousin Emmy's mischief didn't stop there. She "just happened" to bring a pepper shaker, and she "just happened" to spill pepper inside our pillowcases. That night, Jennie and I sneezed our heads off. Mama said we had spring allergies. Our mother changed her diagnosis on wash day when she stripped off our bed linens. Mama's sneezing fit sounded worse than ours.

Emmy's past tricks convinced Jennie and me to take her present threat seriously. This year, April 1 was a Sunday. On Sundays, the relatives always gathered at Grandma and Grandpa's house for dinner.

Jennie and I kept as far away from Emmy as we could. Our big cousin was busy harassing the younger kids, and she pretended that she didn't notice us. But Jen and I weren't fooled. Emmy was like a cat: She loved to toy with her prey before she pounced.

> *"Today's April Fools' Day, Jen! Emmy's up to no good."*

Dinner came straight out of Grandma's kitchen, so Emmy didn't get a chance to tamper with it. But dessert … that was another story.

Grandma had set three platters of home-baked cookies on the sideboard before the guests arrived. Ordinarily, Jennie and I would have gobbled up as many as Mama allowed. Not today! Emmy had had all morning to sprinkle those unattended cookies with salt or pepper—or worse.

My sister and I watched hungrily as Emmy ate the cookies on her plate. But we weren't fooled—nor were our little cousins—and Grandma's baking went largely untouched, at least at the children's table.

Emmy hated to see our cookies go to waste, so little by little, she helped herself to her cousins' desserts. "The cookies must be OK. Emmy's eating them," my sister whispered.

"Today's April Fools' Day, Jen! I guarantee you, Emmy's up to no good. Taste yours if you want. I'd rather starve."

Jennie skipped her cookies.

After dinner, Emmy came over to my sister and me. "Grandma's dessert was dee-lish-us! Too bad you didn't eat any," she said.

Jen and I scowled at our big cousin, but Emmy ignored our dirty looks. "I warned you that I would trick you!" Emmy said.

"Yeah? Well nothing bad has happened, so you lied!" I snapped.

"You big dummy! I April-Fooled you into giving me your cookies!" Emmy snorted.

And so, once again, Emmy had the last word, as she so often did back in the Good Old Days. ❖

April Fool

By Berniece Van Dusen

I gave Central our telephone number and stealthily slid my metal notebook ring around the neck of our black-stem table telephone to hold the receiver down when the operator innocently rang our number. To my delight, Dad rushed into the living room from his hot noon lunch. He had no thought of schoolgirl nonsense or of the day as he called a futile, "Hello! Hello-hello?" into the transmitter, with a puzzled expression.

I was giggling too much to call, "April Fool!"

After that, Mother made several rules. No more telephone jokes. ("A telephone is not a toy. Someone might need the line for an emergency.") No more table tricks, such as switching sugar for salt and vice versa, which had been no end of fun. And we were forbidden to tell an outright lie.

I learned the red-flannel pancake trick when I was too adult to participate. I was boarding in a family of 10 children when I taught in the Catskill Mountains. The oldest son laid a red-cloth circle on the hot griddle and poured batter over it. Then he called upstairs to the next oldest to hurry down for breakfast.

All unsuspecting, the eighth-grader buttered and syruped his cake and cut into it. He sawed away with his knife as he talked, not catching on until he had a bit in his mouth. Then memory came flooding back, and he jumped up, ready to fool the next comer.

It was all right to fold a piece of paper and ask the store clerk, "Do you want to see the funny picture I drew?"

We weren't exactly happy about those hampering rules, but when I pulled a raveling off

Vintage postcard,
House of White Birches nostalgia archives

Mother's dress, and pulled and pulled and pulled some more, until I discovered the unconcealed spool of thread inside her blouse, I forgave her the rules as I wound the thread back onto the spool. Keeping the rules would probably develop our ingenuity.

I should have been suspicious at school when a girl who was no special friend of mine passed me a bag of candy. Treats were usually reserved for best friends, and I wouldn't normally be included in her generosity, but who could resist those chocolate-covered tidbits? Mine had a piece of toothbrush inside. That girl had gone to a lot of trouble and some expense for her disgusting trick.

April Fools' Day didn't end at dark. In the early evening we sisters packed a small change purse with folded paper. We tied on a dark string. Then after carelessly dropping it onto the sidewalk, we hid in the alley between the stores on Main Street.

At first, nobody in that Saturday-night shopping crowd noticed. We had thought nobody could resist a fat pocketbook. When a young lady in the small-town throng finally stooped with her hand out, we jerked the string before she touched the purse. It was such fun to slide it away while calling, "April Fool," though the girl declared to her friends that she had thought it was a hop toad.

Although I've outgrown playing tricks myself, I can still be fooled by the oldest of them all. When a neighbor boy said, "There's a worm on your head," it seemed reasonable since I was sitting under a tree. Maybe adults are the ones to fool because they don't usually get mad or disappointed. They usually laugh good naturedly, probably remembering their own youth. ❖

Dance Around The Maypole

By Lois Bruce

Whatever happened to the May Day festivities of the Good Old Days? When I was 8 or 9, back in the 1930s, and going to grammar school in Phoenix, Ariz., I remember leaving First-Day-of-May baskets on doorsteps and dancing a maypole dance on the school lawn while wearing my best dress and satiny hair ribbon.

The last week in April, our school art class began cutting baskets from pastel construction paper and drawing designs or flowers on them with our crayons. Then we pasted them together with a handle for carrying.

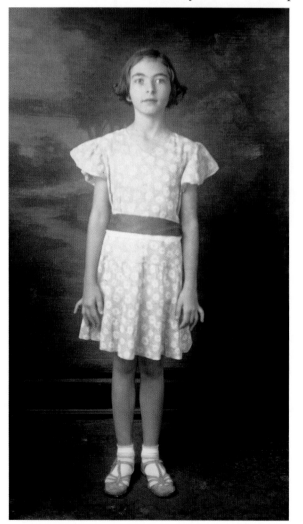

The author and maypole dancer, 1934, 10 years old.

If we were lucky enough to have access to a grassy area, we plucked enough real grass to cover the bottom of the basket. If we had no real grass, we snipped green construction paper to line the basket.

And again, if we had access to flowers (dandelions were acceptable), we picked a handful for each basket we planned to deliver. If not, we drew and colored a rainbow of flowers botanists had never imagined! We carefully cut them out with long, green stems we could drape over the basket. Our prettiest basket was reserved for our mom, along with a hand-made card wishing her a Happy May Day.

The morning of May 1, we gathered our baskets and started walking around the block where we lived, each girl covering a few houses. (Back then, young girls could go walking alone without worrying about crime.) We would dart up the walkway to the door, set a basket down on the porch, ring the bell and run as fast as we could back down the walk. We repeated the process until we had disposed of all our baskets. The residents were supposed to believe fairies had delivered the baskets.

May Day afternoon, we usually took part in a maypole dance on the schoolhouse lawn. We had been practicing all week, each of us holding the end of a different-colored ribbon that was attached to the top of a pole. With careful steps, we skipped around the pole, winding the ribbons in an intricate pattern as we went. If no one goofed, we ended up in a circle at the foot of the rainbow-patterned pole holding the end of our ribbon.

Of course, we hoped for new dresses for our maypole dance, but the Depression was deep in 1934, and money scarce. So we made do with our Sunday best, or more often, our least-worn school dress, washed and stiffly starched. We dreamed of gleaming white shoes, but few had them, so our black or brown school shoes were highly polished, and we danced just as well as if we had worn fluffy dresses and white shoes!

One year, after the maypole was encircled, and we had bowed off the lawn, each girl was given the ribbon she had held during the dance. We were thrilled. Yards of soft, satiny ribbon could be used for all sorts of fancy decorations. I had seen a picture of a canopied bed that looked fit for a princess. I yearned for one, so when I received my blue ribbon, I tied a big bow in its center, fastened the bow to the headboard of my bed and draped the ends down over the sides. It was not precisely a princess bed, but I was immensely happy with it—as I was with bows for my hair and a sash for my dresses and a draped satin gown for my doll. Piece by piece, the ribbon was used until there was nothing left of it but happy memories.

I hadn't thought of May Day in years until I read the notice in a recent *Good Old Days* magazine asking for spring stories. Then I remembered with pleasure and nostalgia those long-ago days. So I got out a calendar and placed a Special Day sticker on the May 1 square. On that day, I will take a few moments to reminisce—and perhaps show the young ones how to make May baskets and become fairies for a morning! ❖

Remembering

By Virginia M. Baty

The giving of May baskets in the town where I lived, Lincoln, Neb., was a tradition that I remember well. Several weeks before May Day, Mother would let my sisters and me help make May baskets for our friends and neighbors. She would make a base pattern from paper and cut it out. The sides could be folded evenly to match. The baskets were small and each had a handle.

To decorate the baskets, Mother would gather 2-inch-wide colored crepe paper on her sewing machine. We would put the gathered crepe paper around the bottom of the baskets and decorate them by pasting lace or cutout designs on the basket sides.

Mother even showed us how to use our fingers to stretch the crepe paper at the top and give it a ruffle effect. The colors were always coordinated: purple with yellow, blue with red, green with pink. No two baskets were alike. They were so beautiful that my young twin sisters wanted to keep them for themselves.

After the baskets were finished, Mother cooked homemade fudge, wrapped each piece in waxed paper and placed several pieces in each basket. Then we added sprigs of lilacs from our big bush in the back yard.

On May Day, we took the filled baskets around to the neighbors, knocked on their door or rang the doorbell, and then hid behind bushes or trees to watch the neighbor pick up the basket.

We never put our name on the baskets, since part of the tradition of giving May baskets was to leave them anonymously. But because our mother was known for her sewing expertise and creativity, neighbors didn't have a hard time recognizing the baskets that came from our house.

Although we no longer give May baskets, I can still see them in my mind's eye. As was so aptly expressed in a quote I read recently, "We do not remember days, we remember moments. Make moments worth remembering." My mother definitely gave me moments worth remembering, including the giving of May baskets on May Day! ❖

May Day! May Day!

By Betty Hatcher

*I*n the 1930s and 1940s, "May Day" didn't remind us of desperate planes and ships shouting an alert. It wasn't about military parades in Red Square or honoring the judicial system in America. Each May Day in my teens, I was up by dawn to wash my face in the dew, a guarantee of beauty. Of course, I really didn't believe that fable. On the other hand, I wasn't going to miss the chance, just in case it did work.

When the calendar said May 1 had arrived, it was the culmination of weeks of work and scores of prayers for good weather wafted aloft by faculty, student body and associated parents of our junior high school. We were all involved in the celebration that fell only slightly lower than Christmas and the Fourth of July, and about equal with Thanksgiving in importance.

From the bleak days of January through March, the hallways were blasted by *Dance of the Flowers* issuing from the band room, competing with the chorus, who harmonized to *Melody in F* with: "Welcome, sweet springtime, We greet thee with song … "

"Welcome, sweet springtime, We greet thee with song ..."

By the time the big day arrived, even the tone-deaf had learned all the words and hummed along.

If you're destined to be tall, as I was, you shoot up a good deal faster than you round out—and you're about as graceful as a newborn colt. It's a struggle not to fall over your own feet on a flat surface. You tower over your slower-growing male classmates, who only have eyes for the short charmers.

So, when parts were assigned annually for the May Day pageant, I had no hope of being chosen Queen of the May, a custom that dates back to antiquity in other countries. The May Queen was always the beauty whose mother kept her hair in golden ringlets. My straight-as-a-board hair alone eliminated me; it couldn't hold a curl for 15 minutes.

No, my hope was to be one of the flowers who crouched in ranks, faces framed by crepe-paper petals of yellow jonquils, purple pansies, pink sweet peas or red tulips. The rest of the year you could tell who had been chosen as flowers because their white gym shoes were dyed green.

Miss Blake, our gym teacher, had an eye for design, and flowers were chosen by height. Who could believe one bloom a foot taller than the others? But, oh, how I wished for green tennis shoes!

Nor could I ever hope to be the West Wind, who floated white gauze scarves as she danced between the crouched ranks to awaken the crepe-paper blooms. She was always the girl who had had real dance lessons.

My last year in junior high school, I was down to one unchewed fingernail when Miss Blake got around to me. "Betty, what are we going to do with you? You're still growing. Well, it's the maypole for you once more." Her hand on my shoulder was kind, but I was doomed to white gym shoes.

Every year, the janitor constructed two 10-foot poles and nailed long strips of pastel cloth to the tops. In three years, my maypole had never wound the ribbons down the pole. Once the apparatus even fell over, to the delight of the audience and to our cha-grin—and the janitor's.

There were no opportu-nities to practice with the actual pole. Our instructions came on the gym floor as we wove in and out around a circle.

It was a strain on us and Miss Blake. The boys were not interested in "this sissy stuff." The girls so chosen were odd shapes and sizes who did not fit the flower ranks and couldn't sing at all. But the only requirement was a white shirt for the boys and a white dress for the girls. Even in the depths of the Depression, we all could meet those standards.

My last May Day celebration dawned clear and bright. Ranks of parents on folding chairs edged the school lawn, and the excitement was noisy. The school band had blown its way through the march that led the Queen of May on the arm of her king to gilded thrones on the school steps. (Even *I* could have been graceful hanging on to *that* jock.)

The chorus wriggled on bleacher tiers center stage and began their song to springtime as the West Wind trailed her scarves between rows of green tennis shoes. It really was effective to see the flower faces lift and stretch upward, reach-ing for the sky.

Finally it was time for the grand finale, the maypoles. As we took our places, I felt the familiar clutch in my stomach. When the band began with a clash of brass, I realized they had switched music on us. Now it was *Country Dances*—and too fast. I eyed Miss Blake, who looked pale as she gave the signal.

Jimmy, the roly-poly redhead in front of me, was waving at his parents behind me. I gave him a punch, which did not turn him in the right direction but brought him an angry step toward me. The boy behind me was treading on my heels, hissing, "Go on!"

A May Day exercise in Bush Park, Salem, Ore., 1914.

Jimmy, never swift to change ideas, finally reversed, but by then the fat girl in front of him was 5 feet away. He ran to catch up, then forgot whether to go inside or out. I skipped forward and bodily shoved him inside. The snickers from parents were louder than the band.

The boy behind passed on my left, and it was my turn to go inside—but there was no one there! It was the same old nightmare I'd fought three years running. The ribbon of pink fabric was wet in my hand, and I felt drops oozing down my armpit.

Forget them all, I told myself and slipped into the rhythm of the gym practices. In and out, in and out I went, surprised to find I was steady on my feet. Jimmy finally had gotten the hang of it, and our circle grew smaller as the pastel strips wound down the pole. Soon the ribbons were so short we were as crouched as the flowers had been at center stage. We dropped the strands and stood.

I glanced at the second maypole. It teetered precariously. The dancers were bunched together on one side, fighting their way through the congestion. Their colored streamers were braiding into one long ponytail that did not involve the pole. The audience convulsed, and the dancers giggled. Band members began to chuckle. When they no longer could pucker for a note, one by one, the instruments faded away. With the last duet of clarinet and tuba, the band director dropped his arms and joined the hilarity. We certainly had greeted "sweet springtime with laughter and song."

I looked up at our neatly braided maypole and the pastel colors smiled at me. At last I had had a part in something that turned out right. When parents began to seek their own, in the confusion before Mom and Dad met me, I felt a hand on my shoulder.

"Betty, you led them beautifully," Miss Blake said. "That's the first time in four years a maypole has succeeded. Thank you."

That was the year I kept my gym shoes white with pride. I was a successful maypole dancer. I'd finally grown up to my feet. Since that day, I've no longer felt I was made up of spare parts.

I miss those May Day celebrations. Something fine and gentle has disappeared from our culture.

Today, that fateful year's West Wind dances on the New York stage. I also see the May Queen in the supermarket sometimes—except now she's Mrs. Five-by-Five. ❖

Vintage postcard, House of White Birches nostalgia archives

May Day

By Mary Masten Kimmel

Oh, welcome,
Maytime, welcome!
We are so glad you've come,
Your bonnet decked with flowers
And your pockets full of sun.

You have brought
a spring bouquet
So dainty and so sweet,
In it, forget-me-nots and
Lady's slippers for your feet.

Your long gown of lacy fern
Has rosettes of wild rose
Stitched with stems of watercress
That you carefully chose.

You passed cold winter weather,
Helped spring along the way,
Arriving here just in time
To celebrate May Day!

The Day Teacher Kissed Me

By Floyd Podoll
as told to his wife, Dorothy Podoll

Back in 1937, I lived in a small town in North Dakota. It was *really* small—150 people! I was born there. Daddy died when I was 6½ years old, leaving just myself, Mother, my paternal grandmother and two younger sisters living in a two-story house. We didn't have much. But we always had enough to eat, and we were always nice and warm. Most of all, I remember how much love flowed in that house.

I thought we were lucky to live in such a small town. We knew everyone, and folks were good to us, helping two widow ladies and three children.

We always looked forward to spring. Winters were harsh in North Dakota. One special spring day back then was May 1, May Day. That day in school, our teacher showed us how to make colorful May baskets. She even brought a little candy to fill each basket.

Our teacher said, "You may take your basket after school, and put it on the doorstep of a special person to you. Knock, then run fast, because if they see you and catch up with you, they will get to give you a kiss." Now, no little boy like me wanted a mushy kiss from a girl!

While our teacher was explaining, I began to think, *She is so nice! Why, one time she even rubbed her gold ring across a sty on my eye, hoping it would help make it go away.* I knew where she lived, and I was certain she could never catch me; I was the fastest runner in my class.

Sure enough, pretty soon I heard my grandma calling, "Sonny, come on out for supper." I knew I had to—and besides, I was hungry.

So off I went after school. I made sure she was home, then I ran up the steps, set the May basket on the step, knocked on the door and started running home.

I thought she wouldn't catch me. But I paused to look behind, and by gosh, there she came, chasing me! I picked up speed when one of my shoes flew off. Oh, boy! But I just kept running, one shoe off and one shoe on.

I made it home past my startled mother and slid under my bed as far as I could get. I heard my mother saying, "Why, come in!" I'm sure she chuckled when she saw the shoe in my teacher's hand and heard the story.

I just lay real still under that bed, hoping that my telltale sister wouldn't give me away. I was there so long I got hungry. I could smell supper cooking. I thought, *Ooh, boy! Did Mother invite my teacher to dinner?* Sure enough, pretty soon I heard my grandma calling, "Sonny, come on out for supper." I knew I had to—and besides, I was hungry.

I came to the kitchen and sure enough, there she was. She said, "Come sit by me." I sat down. She was nice, just as I thought. She didn't tease me, but I did get that kiss on the cheek. Then we bowed our heads in prayer, thanking God for the food we were about to receive.

I will always remember that beautiful spring May Day. And when I grew to manhood and married, our first child was a beautiful little girl—born on May Day! ❖

May Baskets

By Beverly Irwin

*I*t was April, and I needed to get butter cartons and napkins ready for May Day. If I had two butter cartons to cut into halves, I felt extremely lucky. Napkins were not as difficult to find.

I glued crepe paper to cover the outside of each carton half. Next, I crimped strips of crepe paper and twisted them into handles, and again glued them onto the boxes. Sometimes I poked holes in two sides of the box and tied the ends inside. Once in a while, I was able to borrow a staple; that fastened the handles more firmly and more quickly.

After all the butter-box halves were prepared, the paper napkins were next. We didn't use them very often, except for picnics in the summer. They had small, embossed details on their edges.

I would take five to seven of them and start coloring the details as prettily as I could. Then I pulled the top closed with a piece of ribbon, leaving a pouch at the bottom.

May baskets were such a delight. My mother would pop a little popcorn, and if possible, I'd add five or six pieces of candy corn to each box or napkin. If violets, pansies, lilacs or tree blossoms were out, I'd add a sprig to each May basket.

Then the fun began. Our town was fairly small, and the blocks were within easy walking distance. I loaded a small carton with my May baskets and planned the route I'd take to deliver them to my best friends.

Reaching my first destination, I'd knock or ring the doorbell, leave the May basket and hide so that I could watch my friend open the door. Peals of delight rang out when she spotted the May basket. Picking it up, the lucky recipient looked around, trying to spot who might have left it. But there was no one in sight.

Just about then, I would intentionally let my friend see a shoe or dress she'd recognize as mine. Curiosity satisfied, she'd gently close the door, and I was ready to go to the next house on my route.

When I had emptied my carton, I would hurry home to revel in the May baskets that had been left at my door.

The hours I spent making May baskets are but a pleasurable memory now. ❖

1932 *Woman's World*, House of White Birches nostalgia archives

A Beautiful Ritual

By Elizabeth R. Sphar

The day after I'd played April Fool jokes on friends and family, excitement began building again. I was sure I couldn't survive till May 1. For me, May Day was more exciting than Valentine's Day. Of course, I wasn't interested in romance then, so that made a difference.

On May Day, my friends and I gave one another decorated, gift-filled baskets made from brightly colored construction paper or pages from wallpaper-sample books. Fortunately, Father clerked in a store, so he gave me the outdated books. I used them for paper-doll clothes, school notebook covers and sundry other projects, but my major use was for May baskets.

I gave a few pages to "best" friends. This gave me an advantage in guessing who left baskets for me. Half the fun was trying to make my baskets prettier than friends' baskets and different from ones I'd made previous years—no small task, as I gave 20 or more baskets to aunts, uncles and neighbors, as well as classmates.

Most baskets were box-shaped, about 6 x 8 inches, and 6 inches deep. Some were cone-shaped, 6–8 inches deep. All had handles tall enough to slip over doorknobs. I tied ribbons or flowers or both to the handles.

I filled my baskets with candies: gumdrops, jawbreakers, spearmint leaves, licorice babies. I gave special friends homemade fudge or sea foam, which I pestered Mother to make. I often added marbles, jacks, a gaudy ring or a trinket I'd found in a Cracker Jack box.

After dark on May Day, I scurried around our small town, fastening my baskets to doorknobs. Part of the excitement was trying to avoid friends who were also scurrying around, and avoid being seen returning home for another armful of baskets to deliver. We had no fear of being out after dark in those days—and it was *dark*, as there were no porch lights or streetlights and very few cars casting beams along streets. An unwritten law to not have an inside lamp where it would shine on the front doorway was observed by any family hoping for baskets.

We never signed our baskets, so lessons were neglected as we spent days trying to guess the donors of those we received. Boys sometimes spoiled our fun by telling when they'd seen someone leave a basket. They spent their May Day evenings spying on us girls, as they didn't receive or give as many baskets as we girls did.

A few times the boys took the baskets and ate the candies, but as ours was a close-knit community, they were usually satisfied with spying and teasing.

Sooner or later, our egos compelled us to give hints. We wanted friends to know which baskets we'd made, as each was sure her baskets were the prettiest or most unusual. We wanted compensation for the month's work we'd done designing and making them. Close friends guessed donors easily, as they'd glimpsed our papers and ribbons no matter how secretive we tried to be, and they knew our favorite colors. I used wild or common garden flowers in my baskets. so they provided no clue, but the wallpaper often did.

I think it would be fun to revive my favorite childhood ritual of giving May Day baskets to friends and neighbors. Any tradition that expresses friendliness makes our world a happier one.

May baskets filled with colorful spring flowers are a right cheerful expression of neighborliness that adults and children can enjoy. ❖

Mama's Diamond Ring

By Doris R. Gruner

*I*t was the Saturday before Mother's Day in 1932. Daddy had just given each of us a dime with the admonition, "Don't spend it on anything foolish." He had also given us permission to go to Woolworth's five-and-ten around the corner. We lived in New York City. We hurried down the street, clutching our coins tightly. We were on a very important mission: to buy something for Mama for Mother's Day.

A whole dime! None of us had ever had that much money before. We got a penny once in a while, but never a nickel or dime. During the Depression, a dime was to be valued. It could buy food, pay for transportation, or go toward the rent. Parting with three of them was a sacrifice.

We rushed through the door of Woolworth's, and each of us headed in a different direction. We never had been to the store without Mama, but we knew it well. Mama had often taken us with her when she went shopping there. She let us walk around the store while she was making her purchases. We were told to look at things but not touch anything.

> *We urged Mama to sit down and open our gifts and cards.*

Steve, my older brother, then 10, the one with the sweet tooth, headed for the cookie and candy counter. Mama sometimes bought a pound of windmill-shaped spice cookies for 15 cents.

Ronald, 6, lured by the shine and glitter of the jewelry counter, headed there.

I, 8 years old, loved bric-a-brac. I headed to where they sold ornaments, lamps, vases, dishes and the like. As I looked at all the ornaments and statues on the shelves, a helpful saleslady handed things down one at a time so I could examine them. She let me hold each item carefully. Some things cost more than I had to spend.

Then I saw it—a 6-inch statue of the Virgin Mary. The saleslady told me that it was made of plaster and was very fragile. I held it carefully in both hands. It was all cream-colored, even the face and gown, but I knew that Mama would love it. And it cost 10 cents. I gave my dime to the saleslady, and she wrapped the statue in newspaper and placed it in a bag.

Steve found me just as I completed my purchase. He showed me the hard candy he had bought for Mama—the kind he was sure she would like. I told him about the statue, and I promised to show it to him later.

We went looking for Ronald. He was smiling broadly as he turned from the jewelry counter, clutching a small brown bag. Steve and I asked him what he had bought, but he wouldn't tell us.

On the way home, we stopped at the rectory, and Father John obligingly blessed my statue. I thanked him, and we went home.

We rummaged through Mama's paper-and-ribbon bag for something to wrap our gifts. I found a piece of narrow blue ribbon that was just long enough to fit around the base of my statue and tie a small bow.

Steve wrapped his candy in waxed paper, but before closing it completely, he popped a piece into his mouth. He offered one to me and one to Ronald, but we didn't take it. I suggested that he wrap the candy quickly while he still had some to wrap. He chose blue paper, and I helped him tie a bow of yellow ribbon.

I chose pink paper, and Steve helped me wrap the statue in it. We tied it with a piece of bright green cord.

Photo copyright © 2008, www.stockxpert.com

Ronald secretively wrapped his tiny gift, still in its brown bag, in a piece of green paper, and I helped him tie it with green ribbon. He still refused to tell us what it was.

We gave our gifts to Daddy with the Mother's Day cards we had made in school. He told us that he would put the gifts on the table after we left for church. He whispered that he would pick a bouquet of daisies for Mom in the vacant lot at the end of the street.

All through the Mass, the three of us were fidgety, much to Mama's annoyance. It seemed to take forever. We hurried home and burst into our apartment ahead of Mama. Daddy had put Mama's light blue "company" tablecloth on the kitchen table. The daisies were in a green glass vase in the center, and our gifts and cards surrounded the vase. Daddy had set the table for dinner. Everything looked pretty and festive.

Mama hugged and kissed Daddy, and thanked him for the daisies and also for setting the table.

We urged Mama to sit down and open our gifts and cards. Steve handed his to Mama first. She admired and thanked him for the beautiful card he had made. She then opened his gift and complimented him for choosing her very favorite candy.

I handed my gift and card to Mama next. She thanked me for my card and the poem I had written inside. She was surprised when she opened my gift and saw the statue of the Virgin Mary. She was impressed that I had had it blessed by the priest.

Ronald then placed his card and gift in Mama's hands. Steve and I were very curious and watched closely. Mama admired Ronald's card with a big red heart. When she opened his gift, her eyes shone as brightly as the huge solitaire in her hand. She placed it on her finger where it nestled perfectly atop her simple gold wedding ring. It had to be at least a carat of multifaceted glass.

As Mama thanked Ronald, she explained that she had never had an engagement ring and had always wanted one. Now, at last, she had one. Ronald beamed the whole time.

Mama hugged and kissed each of us and thanked us again for our cards and gifts.

The candy was soon gone, as Mama shared it generously with us. The statue, after a few years, was accidentally knocked from Mama's bureau while dusting and was reduced to white powder and small chunks on the bedroom floor.

Only Ronald's ring remained. Mama wore it proudly to church, visiting or other special places. When she wasn't wearing it, she kept it wrapped in her best lace-edged handkerchief in the pin tray on her bureau. Mama treasured that ring, and she wore it for a great many years. I don't know what kept the "diamond" ring sparkling so brightly or how it remained securely attached to its "silver" band.

Yes, it was a genuine "dime-ond" ring, bought for a dime at Woolworth's five-and-ten-cent store. ❖

Mother's Day Carnations

By Joyce Normandin

Years ago, we observed many traditions that now have been dropped by gradual disuse. We always wore a red paper poppy on Armistice Day, and we wore fancy bonnets on Easter. However, the tradition I miss was the one that just about everyone observed on Mother's Day in Brooklyn, and I am sure, in other places. On that day, nearly everyone wore a single white or pink carnation—white in memory of one's deceased mother, or pink in honor of a mother still living.

The day before Mother's Day, Mom and I would take a trip to the florist shop on Seventh Avenue in Brooklyn's Park Slope neighborhood. There, standing in buckets of water, were long-stemmed white and pink carnations. As soon as we opened the door and entered, their sweet aroma beckoned us inside.

We had always purchased one white and two pink carnations for my mother, father and me; my brother, Dennis, was just a baby, so he couldn't wear one. My mother's mom had passed away in 1940. That day in 1943 was a sad one for us, as Dad's mother had passed away the preceding March, and we had to buy him a white carnation instead of a pink.

The author and her mother during the summer of 1942.

When we got home, Mom put the carnations in water. By the time we went out the next day, she had trimmed off the stem, added a matching ribbon, and pinned the appropriate flower to our clothes. I loved to wear that lovely carnation. I often tilted my head toward it to smell its wonderful fragrance.

When we went to church that Mother's Day, every shoulder proudly wore a pink or white carnation on its Sunday best. Florists must have been busy keeping up with all the orders.

I would see my friends, who were all wearing pink carnations. Fortunately, no child I knew had to wear a white one. Since it was after Easter, many of our dresses were in pastel shades.

The boys wore their navy blue suits and sported their carnations in the buttonholes.

We did not need "fashion police" to advise us what to wear. The rules were passed down from generation to generation. White was never worn after Labor Day, and one never wore fur and feathers on the same outfit. We always wore hats and gloves to church on Sundays, and had a clean handkerchief tucked into a small purse or sleeve. Sunday clothes were always our Sunday best, and shoes were polished until they gleamed. Mom used petroleum jelly to shine my black patent leathers.

This ritual of wearing carnations often prompted our parents to tell us stories about our grandparents. Some of the stories were funny, and we laughed. Some told of the hardships they had endured.

We would recall Granny's wonderful cakes, pies, and corned beef and cabbage, and the lovely sewing, knitting and crocheting of Dad's mother. We tucked away these recollections in our memory banks to be passed on to future generations.

As the day wore on, my carnation would begin to show signs of wear and tear as the edges of the petals became discolored and droopy. Then Mom would put all the carnations together in a small, clean baby-food jar and give it to me. I would keep them for another day or two, then press mine between the pages of a favorite book. It was while sorting through some of these old books that I came across a pressed carnation with a slight pink tinge on its now tanned, papery petals. That discovery brought back memories of Mother's Day carnations.

Closing my eyes, I could see the old florist shop on Seventh Avenue, and Mom and me

The author's Grandma Dunn and her mother in Prospect Park, Brooklyn, N.Y.

carefully selecting our flowers. How I wish that tradition would return!

As a child, I could not envision the day when my pink carnation would turn to white. Now, however, I would have to wear a white carnation in honor of my mother. I sometimes buy a pink carnation and put it in a small vase and sniff it every time I pass.

It's my way of remembering a long-ago tradition from the Good Old Days that had a lovely sentiment, a way of honoring mothers who were with us, and of recalling fond memories those who had passed away, but still lived in our hearts. ❖

Photo copyright © 2008, www.stockxpert.com

A Lapful of Flowers

By Mary Neal

I drive to church with a heavy heart. It's Mother's Day, but not like other years, when most of my children came. This year, none will be here, not even a grandchild.

I should be thinking pleasant thoughts—but why have my children treated me so strangely the last two weeks? Why, Linda actually snapped at me yesterday when I called to say I was coming out. "No, you can't come here; I'm too busy." And she didn't say "Happy Mother's Day." I feel unhappy.

Only one card, no calls this morning to wish me a happy day, and David—who usually comes to church—phoned to say, "I can't come. I might see you later."

I park the car, then walk over to the church. My thoughts turn to my oldest daughter, Rachel. I had called her long-distance and she said, "I can't talk now. I'll call back." *Click* went the phone.

But she never called back, and no "Happy Mother's Day." I feel lonely.

In the vestibule I take a bulletin from the greeter and say, "I think I'll go to the office."

But Lyl, the superintendent, who is standing nearby says, "The office is closed. We are meeting in here." Then she quickly moves to the door as if to stop me from going out. When I hesitate, she gruffly adds, "Why don't you find a seat?"

I don't notice a big chair on the platform where the pulpit stood, but I see several rows of seats marked "Reserved." They're probably for the Sunday school kids.

The music stops. I reach down for my purse as I hear Lyl say, "We are honoring one of our mothers today. It will be a surprise to her." *It won't be me,* I think, *for my children aren't here.*

And then I hear it: "Will Mary Neal be escorted to the platform?" Bible, purse—

everything falls from my lap as I take the usher's arm. Then I see the big chair on the platform, and soon I am sitting in that chair, overlooking the crowded church. How I long to have at least one of my children with me!

"Have we got surprises for you!" I hear Lyl say. "The first one is coming through that door."

Out of the office door walks David, my oldest son. He drops a flower in my lap as he hugs me. Then comes Rachel, followed by Linda, Daniel, Ralph and—I can't believe this—Elaine (she lives in North Carolina!). How I hug her, my timid Elaine! Each drops a flower in my lap.

Now, one by one, grandchildren, great-grandchildren and in-laws step through the door. I feel like I'm

> *Now, one by one, grandchildren, great-grandchildren and in-laws step through the door.*

dreaming or seeing things when my two sisters and a niece from Bangor, Maine, are the next to emerge. I almost cry.

Now 35 of my loved ones fill those reserved seats. They have come from Maine, North Carolina, California, Ohio and Michigan. I receive a gift and a certificate recognizing me as "Mother of the Year," and each person there receives a copy of my poems.

As I sit in that chair, overwhelmed by God's love, I have a frightening thought: *How will I feed everyone?* But my children have taken care of that, also. *That's* why I wasn't allowed in their homes; they were cooking for the big day!

We eat later at Ralph's house, and there on his cupboard sits my 40-cup coffeepot, percolating merrily as if to say, "We fooled you!"

Linda says, "I *couldn't* let you come out yesterday; I had a Maine car in the driveway!"

Rachel laughs as she adds, "I was afraid you would hear Elaine's voice, so I hung up the phone."

I'll never forget this happy day. It has taught me never to complain. I feel greatly loved. ❖

Mother's Rosebuds

By Lewis E. Unnewehr

I had settled into a comfortable chair at my son's home after enjoying a delicious Mother's Day dinner, prepared in honor of my wife by my son's family. I was ready to take a short snooze when my grandson wandered in and asked, "What was Mother's Day like when you were young, Grandpa?" I was quite pleased by the question, partly because it was unusual for him to acknowledge that I once had been young. But he also seemed genuinely interested. Nowadays, he said, holidays seem so commercial; he wondered if they had always been like that.

I revived my sleepy spirits a bit to recall some of the holidays I remembered from those ancient 1930s, and I realized there was almost no commercial aspect to any of them. Back then, a whole series of late spring holidays were observed in small Midwestern towns. Some of those holidays are almost forgotten now.

May Day was a quaint, friendly day, long before it was eclipsed by military celebrations in Communist countries. My mother and many others would fill little baskets with spring flowers and wildflowers such as violets, anemones and the mayflowers that seemed to grow in everyone's yards in those days.

We children carried the beautiful, scented baskets to the elderly, shut-in and lonely members of the community.

May ended with Memorial Day, also called Decoration Day, but back then, it was far more than just another three-day holiday weekend. There was a parade, which might feature a fragile Civil War veteran or two. Veterans from the more recent wars marched, usually in uniform, as did the local high-school marching band. If the holiday came on a school day, *Taps* would be played in the school hall on the previous day.

On the Sunday nearest Memorial Day, special music at church was devoted to "the departed" and "souls of the righteous." Then each child in the congregation would be given a flowerpot of red geraniums, and everyone would march single-file to the nearby cemetery to decorate the graves of war veterans. Because I had hay fever, the geraniums' pungent odor would have me sneezing most of the way to the cemetery.

Mother's Day came somewhere in between. It was family centered, and there was plenty of sentiment without the glut of greeting-card advertising that we have today. My mother always said this excessive sentimentality embarrassed her.

There was another flower-related custom in our community. For Mother's Day, everyone was supposed to pin a flower on his or her jacket or blouse, white if one's mother was dead and a colored flower if she were living. My father always pinned several sprays of lily of the valley, his favorite flower, to his suit lapel, which made me sad. I seemed to get stuck with a wilted tulip, which soon lost its petals.

The children presented a big program during the church service, and there was a short sermon glorifying motherhood.

My father, sister and I always prepared the entire Sunday meal on Mother's Day, including cleanup. I'm sure that my mother, realizing that none of us enjoyed meal preparation, was therefore doubly appreciative of our modest efforts. There were no fast foods, no frozen foods, no pizza delivery back then, and we really did prepare the meal from scratch.

"We are Mother's rosebuds, blooming in her heart."

We spent the rest of the day trying to make Mom as happy as possible, giving her the well-intentioned artwork that my sister and I had done in school, singing together, playing games or taking a drive into the country.

I realized I had rambled a bit and that my grandson was getting restless, so I told him I would save Flag Day, Children's Day and the exciting Fourth of July celebrations we used to have for another time. He wandered off into the rec room to watch television.

As the rest of the family socialized while cleaning up the dinner dishes, my thoughts wandered back to a Mother's Day in those unhurried, gentle times before TV, when people still supplied much of their own entertainment. Many churches in that era, late in the Depression, encouraged their young people in the fine arts and gave them ample chances to perform before the congregation on such occasions as Mother's Day.

Our church was on a college campus and had a long tradition of excellent congregational and choral singing. Even primary Sunday school kids were expected to be able to carry a tune, unless they were tone deaf, or to play in the church's small instrumental groups. My family was especially supportive of church music, my father directing the church choir and my mother a frequent soloist.

My sister and I never reached the heights of a Marion Anderson or a Jussi Björling, both of whom got their musical starts in church singing. But we did gain a great love of music, and we learned a lot by participating in musical activities.

I can still hear the tunes of that Mother's Day some 60 years ago, the day I refused to sing. It was the beginning of the end of my childhood.

My aunt, who ran the Sunday schools, set up the program, and as usual, my sister and I were expected to perform. I was in the sixth grade and still had a nice, clear soprano voice (and had, in fact, just performed the second lead in an operetta at school). I was given a solo, *Mother, I Love You*, to sing as the closing number. I learned the song easily; I can still go through it in my mind, though I have never heard it since. That kind of song must have gone out of style years ago.

We went through several rehearsals, and then, suddenly, about a week before the program, I decided that I did not want to sing. I used all sorts of excuses—I was too old, too big (I never admitted to being fat) … Aunt Freda's two boys, my cousins, didn't have to sing (I knew they couldn't carry a tune in a basket) so why should I? … I didn't feel good … and so on.

But basically, it was one of those adolescent rebellions, a realization that I wasn't a little boy anymore. I felt that no one appreciated me. I expected a lot more pleading and even bribing.

My mother looked hurt when I expressed my childish complaints, but she said, "Well, I won't force you." And then Aunt Freda heard about a new family in the church whose children did some singing; maybe they would pitch in.

Mother's Day arrived. I sat alone in the balcony to show my disdain for this "kid stuff," and to see how much I would be missed. My parents were in the choir loft in the front of the church.

My sister started the program with a nice piano rendition of *Songs My Mother Taught Me* by Dvorak. Then some of the little Sunday school kids performed a few songs, including the usual shuffle-and-step actions.

A high-school girl read an essay on "Mothers in the Bible," and a boy read one of those sentimental Irish poems about mothers. A classmate of mine played a clarinet solo, accompanied by my sister. I thought, *What a corny program!*

I was to have been next, but in my place, out came the three Mutersbaugh children. The oldest, a girl about my age, stood in the middle, her arms around a younger brother and sister at each side, and their mother came out to play the piano.

They were handsome children, dressed in their best Sunday clothes, not a hair out of place. They stood with angelic smiles as their mother played the introduction.

Then they sang, in perfect three-part harmony, a song that haunted me for months afterward. There were several verses, each followed by a lilting chorus that began: "We are Mother's rosebuds, blooming in her heart." With their healthy, rosy cheeks, they actually looked like little rosebuds, and I immediately fell in love with the oldest girl; according to the church bulletin, her name was Alice.

I looked down on the congregation. Half of them, male and female alike, were wiping their eyes. Every time the kids came to that chorus, I felt like a piece of crabgrass in front of those "rosebuds." I looked at my mother, and she smiled at me, a slightly sardonic smile that said what an opportunity I had lost—and I knew it.

There was a hush in the congregation as the closing lines of the tune reverberated through the sanctuary. The preacher finally got up and gave a hasty benediction, and I'm sure I detected a cracking in his voice.

The Mutersbaugh kids were the darlings of the church and community for a year or so. I never got to pursue my attraction to Alice since she went to a different school, and the family moved away within two years. And that was my last chance to sing as a boy soprano, for my voice soon started to change, and I did more croaking than singing for the next several years.

I felt guilty about refusing to sing for my mother, and I knew that I had hurt her that day. She said very little about it, and we all enjoyed a good dinner cooked by my father, but a cherished moment had been lost.

And it was a loss that has stayed with me all my life. ❖

M-O-T-H-E-R

Lyrics by Howard Johnson
Music by Theodore Morse
(Originally published in 1915)

I've been around the world, you bet,
but never went to school
Hard knocks are all I seem to get,
perhaps I've been a fool;
But still, some educated folks,
supposed to be so swell,
Would fail if they were called
upon a simple word to spell.
Now if you'd like to put me to the test,
There's one dear name
that I can spell the best!

"M" is for the million things she gave me
"O" means only that she's growing old
"T" is for the tears she shed to save me
"H" is for her heart of purest gold
"E" is for her eyes with love-light shining
"R" means right and right she'll always be
Put them all together they spell MOTHER,
A word that means the world to me.

When I was but a baby,
long before I learned to walk,
While lying in my cradle,
I would try my best to talk;
It wasn't long before I spoke
and all the neighbors heard,
My folks were very proud of me
for "Mother" was the word.
Although I'll never lay a claim to fame,
I'm satisfied that I can spell the name:

"M" is for the mercy she possesses
"O" means that I owe her all I own
"T" is for her tender, sweet caresses
"H" is for her hands that made a home
"E" means ev'rything
she's done to help me
"R" means real and regular, you see
Put them all together they spell MOTHER,
A word that means the world to me.

Dinner on The Grounds

By Jerry C. Smith

The title is right—"grounds" is supposed to be plural, and "dinner on the grounds" was on the grounds of the church. When folks actually eat on the ground, it's called a picnic. Dinner on the grounds was always the high spot of our church year. However, since our Birmingham congregation didn't do that, we had to load up the car and drive to Mom's ancestral church on Sand Mountain, near Albertville, Ala.

It was officially named Freeman Chapel Congregational Methodist Church, but everyone knew it simply as Freeman. Each year at Mother's Day, Freeman was the site for dinner on the grounds, visited by many whose forebears had left Sand Mountain generations earlier. My great-grandfather, Med Sparks, gave the land for the church, was its first pastor, and insisted it be named for the first congregant who died rather than for himself.

Each year at Mother's Day, Freeman was the site for dinner on the grounds.

In the early 1950s, Freeman had neither electricity nor running water. All the church's doors and windows stood wide open, allowing easy access to May breezes, as well as bugs, unruly children taking shortcuts, and even an occasional lost dog. The restroom was a nice, new, concrete-block four-holer out behind the church. It replaced the old wooden privy that hadn't survived a windstorm.

Cars would start pulling into the sandy, oak-shaded lot at about 9 o'clock every second Sunday morning of May, and the fellowship began immediately. Hugs and kisses were mandatory—and the curse of all us youngsters because all the elderly people either chewed tobacco or dipped snuff in those days. We'd dirty many a handkerchief wiping off those awful brown rings.

Mother's Day services involved a lot of singing, so loud that you didn't have to be indoors to enjoy it. However, the choir was deficient in bass and baritone voices because the menfolk preferred to gather outside in the shade, usually around the newest car on the lot. Their own fellowship included looking at car engines, telling war stories, whittling, spitting, kicking sand and smoking roll-your-owns.

True to its name, Sand Mountain soil was mostly brownish yellow sand, just the thing for us kids to get in our shoes and on the floorboards of the family car. Where you have sand, you also have ant lions, weird little critters with huge pincers that make conical pits in the sand to trap ants. We spent lots of time dibbling in their lairs with pine straws, trying to entice the tiny monsters to the surface.

Giant oak trees shaded the entire lot, and the ground was littered with acorns the size of our father's thumb. They were just the thing for whittling miniature pipe bowls, and a nearby canebrake provided stems.

Sometimes an understanding adult would give us a pinch of cigarette tobacco from his little cloth bag, just to watch us light up and then turn green from the fumes of the uncured acorn.

Sometime near noon, a call would go out for the men to begin taking the church pews outdoors. These were arranged front-to-front to form wide tables, with the opposing backs making perfect windbreaks.

Then car trunks were opened, and the ladies brought out a bewildering variety of delicious Southern foods to place on the starched white tablecloths spread upon our makeshift buffet.

Each of these proud women had a special dish. We watched as folks jockeyed for starting positions nearest their favorites just before the blessing was given.

The variety was endless, and somehow they always knew what everyone else was going to bring so we didn't wind up with all potato salad. This wonderful fare was cooked in the traditional country way, and there wasn't a KFC tub in sight. It was all original, the real thing.

We're talking fried chicken, fresh-caught river catfish, green beans with new potatoes, corn on the cob, a vast array of baked beans, potato salads and coleslaw, candied yams, deviled eggs, turnip greens, collards, field peas, okra, marinated salads, mashed potatoes with real lumps, macaroni and cheese, chili, homemade biscuits, corn bread, Aunt Hazel's peerless sweet iced tea made with iron water, and

enough indescribably delicious desserts to feed a Confederate regiment. Occasionally, someone even remembered to bring napkins.

Dinner was eaten from paper plates with wooden forks, usually on the fender of a car. Third helpings were commonplace and expected. After all, a lot of this food would not survive the hot trip back home, so why not gorge ourselves, lest the other pigs back on the farm eat it instead?

After-dinner activities centered on the cemetery as relatives admired the flowers they had placed shortly after arrival and caught up on who had done what with whom since last May.

Dinner on the grounds, Freck, Ark. Photo courtesy Doretha Dillard Shipman.

Many tears were shed over graves, more so by those who could recall when this lot was not so full. The founding families of Freeman were a close bunch of folks.

Since my childhood, I've been back to Freeman many times for Mother's Day, and also on weekdays when no one else was there. I've walked the quiet graveyard alone and heard lingering sounds of better days somewhere beyond the time horizon. Many of Freeman's markers belong to folks whose pall I've borne; people we all considered immortal—until they died.

What I wouldn't give for a 5-minute chat with any of them, mainly to apologize for not visiting more often when they were alive. ❖

Glorious Days of Summer

Chapter Two

The glorious days of summer were headlined by several patriotic holidays, but none quite as important to a kid as Independence Day. A July can't roll around without my thoughts turning to the Independence Days of my youth. Those were times when *everybody* had a holiday, and *everybody* celebrated the birth of our nation.

We kids always had enough plans to fill three Fourths of July, and we expected to do it all in just over 12 hours. Mama and Daddy, on the other hand, had a better grip on reality and had already made sensible plans for the day.

For many years we had a summertime ritual for the holiday. The year I remember best was when I was about 10. We drove to the Jones' home by midmorning and then headed to the creek. I'm sure our families made quite a sight—four adults and eight youngsters all piled into the front, back and sides of the Jones' pickup truck.

Bear Creek had a great swimming hole. Usually several families would gather there for the holiday, and the creek would end up as one big social event. There was plenty of water fun before mothers called everyone out for lunch. Lunch was standard country fare: fried chicken, potato salad, green beans, peas and new potatoes from the garden. A grape Nehi soda—we didn't get those except on special events—capped off the meal. Then dessert was homemade ice cream, hand-cranked right there on the creek bank. There was nothing like the outdoors to make that Fourth of July picnic taste better than just about anything!

We were admonished not to go back into the water for a while after eating (for fear of cramps), so we used the opportunity to light off the few firecrackers we had purchased. We took our firecrackers down to the low-water bridge. We lit and threw them along the bank, sometimes getting them close enough for the girls to squeal—and that made it all the more fun. The folks usually just laughed and called our little fireworks display the candles on America's birthday cake.

> *We lit America's birthday candles and celebrated with gusto back in those glorious days of summer.*

The afternoon was punctuated with as much swimming, laughter and shenanigans as a bunch of kids could put into one summer day.

As the late afternoon sun dipped behind the hills, we were summoned from the clear stream again, this time for cold watermelon. In the dusk, Daddy or someone would produce a guitar, and we would serenade the approaching nighttime, not willing to let the holiday end.

But end it did. Clambering into the back of the truck, we lay on our backs, watching for Fourth of July shooting stars in the evening sky. We always fell asleep on the way home.

Even at our young age, I think we realized that the birthday of our nation was more than just any other day. We had the freedom to go to the creek; to eat what our parents had earned by the sweat of their brows; to sleep peacefully in a world that didn't know much peace. And we thanked God for the country He had blessed with such freedom.

In the Good Old Days, we remembered what the Fourth of July was all about. We lit America's birthday candles and celebrated with gusto back in those glorious days of summer.

—Ken Tate

Decoration Day

By Venus E. Bardanouve

Certain days stood out gloriously when I was a little girl! There were Christmas, Easter, Halloween, Fourth of July—and Decoration Day. That holiday is now called Memorial Day, but when I was a child, it was Decoration Day. Our town made much of this day of remembrance of our soldiers, and we children were an important part of the celebration. We participated in the parade—girls wore white dresses and boys white shirts as we carried flowers to be placed on the graves of veterans. Our yards had yielded tulips, bridal wreath, lilac, peonies and other spring flowers for the bouquets to decorate the graves of those we were honoring.

> *We were filled with patriotism, and everyone carried flags.*

The parade began at the courthouse and marched down our short main street. At the head of the procession, following the soldiers with the flags, was a Model T Ford in which "Grandaddy" Ware and a couple of other Civil War veterans rode. The brass buttons on their worn old uniforms were polished to a high shine, and the people on the street clapped for them as they rode past.

I was especially proud of them because Grandaddy Ware was our neighbor. Knowing him so well made me a bit special for that moment too.

There were a few men who had been in the Spanish-American War. The ones I remember most clearly, however, were those handsome younger men who had fought in World War I.

Some of their uniforms were beginning to be a bit tight, but they still looked grand to us as they proudly marched down the street.

We were all filled with patriotism, and everyone carried flags. Ladies from the auxiliaries of the Daughters of the Veterans and American Legion shepherded us children with our flowers and flags. As I walked along on the pavement in my stiff, white organdy dress, I was sure our country was the greatest in the world, and I felt I was a real part of it.

Our goal was the cemetery. It was about 3 miles out of town, so after parading for a few blocks, we children were herded into cars and driven the rest of the way. The soldiers marched the full distance.

When we reached the military circle in the center of the cemetery, we children were dispersed with the bouquets, which we were to put on every veteran's grave. We knew which graves were those of veterans because each had a small flag inserted in a bronze marker at the head of the grave.

The weather was balmy in late May in Nebraska. I don't remember there ever being a rainy Decoration Day—it would not have dared to rain. We gathered in the military circle at 11 a.m. for a ceremony that included singing, speeches and the traditional mournful taps.

Then we gathered in the Legion Hall for a patriotic program. We children had learned wartime songs in school, so when the crowd sang *Over There* or *Pack Up Your Troubles* from World War I or even *When Johnny Comes Marching Home Again* from the Civil War, we joined in heartily.

We all had to learn *The Gettysburg Address, In Flanders Fields* and other such readings in school, and some students were chosen to recite these tributes at the afternoon program. There were speeches, too, but somehow they have gone from my memory. I'm sure they were inspiring and patriotic, though, because we all believed that "the war to end all wars" had been fought not too many years before!

Then came the day when the old soldiers of the Civil War were no longer among the marchers. The Depression cast a pall over our lives, and Decoration Day as a day for decorating the graves of veterans was gone.

We now celebrate Memorial Day with newer wars and veterans to remember, and we honor all our dead—not just veterans—on that day. Little towns no longer celebrate quite as wholeheartedly. We do remember our soldier dead with honor, but we have discovered to our regret that the war to end all wars, celebrated once by young and old alike, was not really that.

But in my memory, when the end of May draws near, I see children in white dresses and white shirts solemnly placing spring bouquets on the graves of those who gave their lives so that freedom may be ours. ❖

In Flanders Fields

By Lt. Col. John McCrae, M.D.
(1872–1918) Canadian Army

In Flanders Fields the poppies blow
Between the crosses row on row,
That mark our place; and in the sky
The larks, still bravely singing, fly
Scarce heard amid the guns below.

We are the Dead. Short days ago
We lived, felt dawn, saw sunset glow,
Loved and were loved, and now we lie
In Flanders fields.

Take up our quarrel with the foe:
To you from failing hands we throw
The torch; be yours to hold it high.
If ye break faith with us who die
We shall not sleep, though poppies grow
In Flanders fields.

Yesteryear Memorial Day

By Marylyn Chapman

"How much you've grown, and how much you look like your mother!" By the time I was 9 years old, I was used to this yearly greeting when my parents met their friends at Pleasant Hill Cemetery, Lime Springs, Iowa.

The holiday for which we gathered was called Decoration Day in the 1930s, and it was an important spring ritual for our family. We made the 50-mile trip to visit my parents' relatives and school friends, and to pay homage to deceased relatives and war veterans.

The date was always May 30, regardless of the day of the week. Sister and I rejoiced because school was out, and perhaps we had new dresses and new white buckle sandals—a budget stretch some years during the 1930s.

We always hoped for a sunny day, and we always watched for certain flowers to blossom in Dad's garden. It was my job to cut long branches of white spirea, iris of many colors, and the grand red, pink and white peonies, which were my favorites. We plunged them into tubs of water in our basement to await their ride north with us.

Even today, their fragrances remind me of those trips. We drove straight to the cemetery and mingled our flowers with others in large tubs. These were to be shared among the graves later. Mother instructed Dad in the careful, yearly planting of the red geraniums and ferns she always brought for our grandparents' graves.

The high-school band tuned up their instruments for the parade. Often a veteran would join their ranks. At some secret signal, the adults gathered their children close, and we became a congregation huddled under stately trees.

The minister intoned his very long prayer. Flies pestered our sweaty faces and legs while we tried to stand still in the humidity. Finally came the thankful "Amen."

Then it was parade time. First came the color guard; next, any veteran who could walk up and down the hillsides to salute and pay homage to fallen comrades. After the band came the children, carrying bunches of dripping flowers.

We marched together up and down the rows, laying our flowers at the headstones of veterans whose graves were adorned with small, new American flags.

My father walked among the men as a World War I veteran, giving his salutes.

Some veterans wore ill-fitting military jackets; others paraded in shirtsleeves with their campaign ribbons and medals proudly affixed. An old military cap or Legion hat topped off their uniforms of the day. Great-Grandfather Isaac B. Howland, a Civil War veteran, always received some of my favorite pink peonies.

The mournful sound of taps and the salute of rifle shots echoed across humid cornfields. Old soldiers never flinched at the sounds. Children covered their ears. Others wore tears on their cheeks.

As the ceremony ended, the adults shouted and waved their goodbyes, corralling the children who were now galloping among the graves. There were kisses all 'round and more pats on the head for me, many from unknown adults whom we always addressed as "Aunt" or "Uncle." Soon we were herded toward waiting cars and were on our way to a relative's farm to enjoy heaps of home-cooked food. Possibly there would be a pickup softball game to keep afternoon boredom away, with lemonade and extra sugar cookies from Mother's Aunt Mary.

Then, at the end of the day, a stop at Grandma Jones' farm often included late-afternoon pie before we headed home. ❖

Fruit Jars and Lilacs

By Donna M. Bosman

This time of year always takes me back in memory to the Memorial Days of the 1940s. Grandma Williams was the matriarch when it came to gathering her family at the Gladstone Hotel in Fargo, where she and Grandpa were landlords. All of us being together at that time was one of the few constants we could count on in those days. We would all meet to decide what would be planted on the resting places of not only immediate family, but of aunts and uncles whose families had moved away.

One week before Memorial Day, the flowers, tools and a big picnic lunch were packed into the trunk of the car.

The last thing Grandma would do before we left for the cemetery was head for the vast rows of beautiful purple lilacs that flanked Uncle Chris' house in the country. She'd say, "We can't forget the fruit jars and lilacs!" Then, after she snapped off a large bouquet, we'd be on our way.

Eight of us—Grandpa, Grandma, Mom, Aunt Alma, her two little daughters, Uncle Chris and me—packed ourselves into the car, with the littlest ones sitting on laps. We all squeezed in together "like a can of sardines," Grandpa would say. Then we'd travel out to the old country cemetery. The adults planted flowers around the stones and pruned the bushes. I helped by carrying a sprinkling can with water to whoever was doing the planting. Grandpa would use his jackknife to cut grass away from the footstones.

Grandpa would use his jackknife to cut grass away from the footstones.

The last thing they'd do was scrub the stones to remove all evidence of the numerous birds that had also found rest in that place.

Finally our labors of love were completed. We'd wash the tools at the water faucet, dry them and put them back in the trunk. Then Grandpa would lift out our picnic lunch and carry it to the long stone table beside the "winter holding building."

"Time to eat! Come on kids, sit up!" Mother shouted. Each bite of lunch would be punctuated with reminiscences of bygone days when our loved ones were still among us.

I listened to these conversations. Their chats recalled the funny times and the habits they'd had. Once I heard someone say, "He'd roll over in his grave if he knew you planted bachelor buttons on it! He was allergic to them!" Humor was alive and well, even among the more solemn moments. Remembering them—that was the important thing. I realized later in life that I had retained a lot of what I'd heard about those family members.

Always before leaving those consecrated grounds, we'd walk over and take one last glance at the resting places, noting how pretty they looked now that we'd done our work. Grandma spoke softly at one grave and explained to me that it was my Uncle Olaf, her 26-year-old son. In my innocence, I asked, "How come you're talking to him? Can he hear you?"

"Oh, yes," she answered with a smile, "he can hear me. He can hear me."

With our tummies full and our job well done, we all walked to the car and climbed in—all except Grandma. I heard her say, "I almost forgot." She went to the trunk, then walked over to the water faucet where she filled a blue canning jar with water. She placed a beautiful bouquet of slightly limp purple flowers in it and set it next to Uncle Olaf's headstone. As she got in the car, she said, "I almost forgot the lilacs!"

As time rolled on and families relocated, the annual planting was neglected. But someone always made sure that there were always "fruit jars and lilacs" flanking the stones, and the children learned that our loved ones in that place would always be with us as long as we kept them in our hearts. ❖

Olga Williams, the author's grandmother and organizer of the family cemetery's Memorial Day beautification projects.

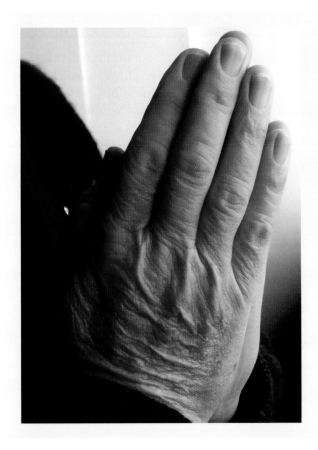

My Father's Hands

By Alice Saunders Mason

My father's hands were hard and rough
From work he did from dawn to dusk.
He tore from hills' reluctant sides
The roads over which smooth traffic glides.
No stream too wide has bridge to span,
Up rocky cliffs go roads he planned.
To him, machinery was a joy
He knew, as a child knows his toy.
The harder the problem that tried his mind,
The better he liked it, and covered with grime
And satisfaction from a hard day's toil,
He cared not that his hands were soiled.
Ah! Tender and gentle were my father's hands,
To the child he loved—and who loved this man.

Photo by Adrian van Leen, courtesy www.sxc.hu

Family Tradition

By Dorothy Camp Berryman

When I was a child in the 1930s, before holidays were moved to the Monday after the event so that people could have a long weekend, one of my favorite holidays was May 30. We did not call the holiday Memorial Day then; we called it Decoration Day. It not only signaled the beginning of summer, but included events that taught me early on to accept the cycle of life. And I recall a family tradition concerning that observance that started when I was about 10 years old and continued until my father's death when I was 16.

My parents, two sisters and I would leave the house early on that day. We piled into Dad's old Ford and drove from Chicago's North Side to our first stop at Oak Ridge Cemetery on the western rim of the city. There we paid our respects to deceased family members, Grandpa, Grandma and Great-Grandma.

As we placed flowers on their graves, Dad said, "Grandpa bought this eight-grave plot in 1920 for the handsome sum of $100." He told us how Grandpa Bill had met Grandma—Melissa Lambert, a young widow with two small children—and married her, then brought the family, including Melissa's mother, Cynthia, to Chicago from their home in Tennessee.

"'Sinthie,' as Great-Grandma was called, lived to be 90 years old," Dad said. "She died in her rocking chair on the front porch while puffing on her corncob pipe. Let that be a lesson to you girls!" he chuckled. "Don't smoke!"

Mother Mary (right) and Aunt Josephine (center) are working with a friend, cleaning up after a picnic in 1932 while the men rest.

I once asked Dad why he took the name Camp instead of Lambert. He answered, "It was to respect Grandpa for taking on the responsbility of the father who died when I was a baby. By the way, someday Grandpa's second wife, Mona, will probably be buried here too. If so, Grandpa will rise between two wives on Resurrection Day. I wish him luck!" Then he said, "Eventually, your mother and I will rest here too. We hope you girls will not forget us on Decoration Days to come." We have not forgotten.

Our next stop was just down the road at Mount Carmel Cemetery. There we visited the graves of a few more relatives.

Unlike some modern burial grounds with their unobstructed views and small bronze markers, Mount Carmel was a jumble of granite and marble statuary. There were also many private mausoleums, including those of some of Chicago's most notorious gangsters. Some headstones even had photographs of the deceased embedded in them, covered with bubbles of glass.

One grave in particular held our attention when Dad told the story of its occupant. The inscription read "Dion O'Banion."

"You see," Dad said, "O'Banion owned a flower shop in Chicago during the 1920s. On the surface he was a hail-fellow, but actually his shop was a front for his bootlegging business. He was a big shot until 'Scarface' Al Capone came to town.

"Then one day, a couple of O'Banion's pals came to the flower shop. When he extended his hand, they answered with a hail of bullets. It seems that they had gone over to the enemy.

"Dion's murder was never officially solved," Dad said, "but I guess there was room for only one boss in Chicago gangland, 'Scarface' Al Capone." Mother stopped Dad before he could tell us how Capone got his scar.

At that point in the story, there seemed to be a sudden gust of wind and a creaking sound. Was it a vault opening? footsteps? We jumped. Could it be O'Banion's ghost—or even Scarface himself lurking nearby? How exciting! Who needed Dracula?

After a last look back at the past, we returned to the car and a date with the future. We headed north again on the long drive to Edgebrook Forest Preserve. We liked to spend the rest of the day at the picnic grove with friends and other relatives. Dad joined his cronies for a game of horseshoes or checkers. Mother chatted with friends as they piled food upon long wooden tables. We kids headed for the shallow creek, a tributary of the then-unpolluted Des Plaines River.

We changed into our bathing suits in a wooden shack that Mother called "the facility" and Dad called "the outhouse." Whatever it was, we left its malodorous confines quickly.

Our bathing suits were made of itchy wool and had attached skirts. It was a good thing that the creek was shallow in most spots because the suits were heavy when wet and could have presented a drowning hazard in deep water.

However, if we looked up, we could see that there was always a mother, grandmother or aunt watching us as we frolicked in the water. Usually it was Dad's sister, our Aunt Josephine, the informer. We felt safe under her stern gaze. Only much later did we learn that she could not swim a stroke. Soon a voice would come from where the tables were set up. "Lunch is ready! Come and get it! Last one here gets leftovers!"

"We hope you girls will not forget us on Decoration Days to come."

We gorged ourselves on Mother's baked beans, Aunt Josephine's coleslaw and the food that others had brought: potato salad, ham, freshly baked bread and wedges of apple pie. Afterward, the men relaxed while the women cleared the tables. Those who wished could then play pinochle or penny ante.

We sisters changed clothes again and played games with other children until all of us were tired enough to sit in a circle on the ground and tell ghost stories. I was well prepared: "See, there was this fellow, O'Banion …"

At dusk, Dad brought out his harmonica, and soon the air was filled with the sweet sound of *Golden Slippers* or *Moonlight Bay*. Then a guitar would pick up the melody and voices would join in on many old favorites.

From a nearby group of strangers, a fiddle gave us a bouncy reel, and people drifted toward the dance pavilion in the glade. For a little while, friends and strangers alike joined hands and clicked heels in merry claps and steps.

Gradually, headlights came on, and folks could be heard packing up or carrying sleepy children to cars. One by one, taillights grew dim on the road leading out of the park.

A few last shouts of goodwill, one or two final honks of a horn, and it was the end of another perfect Decoration Day. ❖

Memorial Day Snow of 1947

By Joyce Tintjer

*S*chool was out for the summer, the crops were planted, and was I ever excited! Over that Memorial Day in 1947, we would be taking a family vacation, an almost unheard-of event. I had never been on a vacation before. We were going to stay in a cabin by a lake for three whole days! I had just turned 8 and was living on our family farm south of Melbourne, Iowa, with my parents and three older sisters. My two brothers, the eldest of my siblings, were out on their own, so only the six of us would be going.

Our vacation destination was Lake Okoboji, in the northwestern corner of the state. It seemed like light-years away to me, since I'd never been more than 30 miles from home. My favorite cousin, Shirley, and her family were going, too, so I was beside myself with anticipation of all the fun we'd have together.

We kids packed swimsuits, shorts and short-sleeved shirts. Mom had enough foresight to add long pants and light jackets to the mix. She knew that early mornings at the lake could be a little cool.

> *We kids didn't want to leave, especially me. After all, this was our first vacation.*

On the trip up, we stopped at a truck stop for lunch, another new experience for me. I don't remember ever eating out before.

The closer we got to our destination, the more we bugged Mom and Dad. "How much farther? Aren't we about there yet?"

We finally arrived and got settled at Smitty's Cabins, with side-by-side accommodations for my family and Shirley's. While Mom cooked the evening meal, we kids explored the lakeshore. It was difficult to get to sleep that first night after all the new things I'd experienced. But at long last, I fell asleep.

The next morning, it wasn't merely chilly—it was downright cold. And we had no heat! Mom trundled us kids next door to my cousin's cabin because theirs came with a small heater.

The unexpected weather called for a major decision: whether to stay, or pack up and go home. Of course, we kids didn't want to leave, especially me. After all, this was my first vacation. Finally, the grown-ups decided that since we were already there and paid up for three days, we might as well stay. Besides, the cold probably wouldn't keep the fish from biting. We kids cheered our approval.

Arnold's Park, a nearby amusement center, had just opened for the season, but so few people were there because of the cold snap that the only thing open was the roller-skating rink. Mom and my aunt figured that would be something for us kids to do to keep us out of the cold. And what fun it was! We kids had the rink all to ourselves!

This was another first for me: shoe skates. At home, I had a pair of skates that clamped onto my shoes, and our only "rink" was a rough cement slab in the cattle lot. Since I wasn't a strong skater, my greatest accomplishment was staying on my feet instead of my backside. But with so few skaters, I was able to hone my meager skills.

After an entire afternoon at the rink, a big surprise awaited us upon leaving the building. It was snowing! And not just a few flurries, but big, wet flakes coming down like a small blizzard. By the time we got back to our cabins, there was 4 inches of snow on the ground.

Still hard-pressed to find activities to keep six rambunctious kids occupied, our moms chose the movies. At least it should be warm. A small theater in the nearby town of Milford was playing *The Jungle Princess*, starring Dorothy Lamour. To this day, I have fond memories of that movie. For years afterward, Shirley and I relived the scenes of the movie in our play.

After the movie, we all crowded into the one heated cabin. We kids had a blast staying overnight with our cousins. The next morning, we packed, and they drove us back to the comforts of home.

The corn had grown several inches by then. The leaves got nipped by the cold, but most of the plants survived. The soybeans hadn't yet emerged, and that was a lucky thing since they're more sensitive to the cold. So for my parents, the worst of the unseasonable snowstorm was a ruined family vacation.

But it wasn't ruined for me. In fact, it stands out vividly in my memory as one of the most fun events of my childhood. An entire roller-skating rink to ourselves. How lucky could we be? And seeing *The Jungle Princess*, the best movie of my childhood. And snow, at any time of the year, is special when you're only 8 years old! ❖

Farewell to a Winter's Friend by John Slobodnik, © House of White Birches nostalgia archives

Hometown Parades

By Madeline J. Huss

I recently read an article that listed the best parades in the United States. It included the Disney parade, Macy's Thanksgiving Day Parade and the Rose Bowl Parade. These and other large parades celebrated throughout the United States are spectacular indeed. And yet, they can't quite capture the thrill and excitement I experienced as I watched parades in my hometown when I was a young girl.

On holidays such as Memorial Day and the Fourth of July, the whole town looked forward to these events. The school band provided the music. Baton twirlers proudly marched behind. Flags waved bravely as practically every organization in town contributed its contingent of marchers. The VFW, the American Legion, the Amvets, the Elks, the Masons—all were included.

We also had firemen's parades. Volunteer firemen from all over the country marched proudly down the middle of town when it was our turn to sponsor the event.

The music was louder at these parades, as each unit brought its own band to accompany the fire engines that rolled slowly along the parade route, their clanging bells announcing their approach. Crowds lined the sidewalks for all the parades, pushing baby carriages and setting up folding chairs for the elderly.

The earliest parades I remember included veterans from World War I wearing their uniforms and all their insignia. There were even some veterans of the Spanish-American War, but they were few in number and mostly wheelchair-bound.

After the Japanese bombed Pearl Harbor and World War II began, I began to realize what war really meant. Each year, a small but steady number of wounded veterans from World War II joined the marchers. They were young—not much older than we teens who watched the parade. Some of them were our relatives, friends and neighbors.

I remember the jubilant parade of 1946, the year after the war ended. Veterans of the conflict

The band marches on during one of the hometown parades.

arrived home daily from foreign shores. That Memorial Day, all the returning GIs joined in the celebration. The parade extended for several blocks as they marched smartly to loud cheers from the crowd gathered to honor them. Flags flipped gaily in the breeze. Each and every one of us was proud to be an American.

Many towns no longer celebrate holidays with parades. I am sad to think of those who would have joined them—veterans of the Korean conflict, the combatants who served in Vietnam and the Gulf War, and the latest conflicts in Afghanistan and Iraq. Even though they no longer march in their hometowns, they still deserve tribute and honor for serving our country in time of need. ❖

Good Old Memorial Days

By Carol Schneider

In my hometown in central Utah, something special has been lost from the Memorial Day weekend. Years ago, it was a time for families to gather and remember their departed loved ones. It was a time to reminisce, shed a few tears, catch up on family happenings and renew old ties. Preparations began during the winter months. In 1938, when I was 8 years old, Mother taught me the art of making beautiful paper flowers for decorating family graves.

Patterns for different flower petals and their leaves were cut from cardboard. Using the pattern, Mother cut stacks of flower petals and leaves from a rainbow of colored crepe paper.

She taught me to shape a variety of flowers—roses, carnations and tulips were her specialties. The flowers were fastened with thin wire shredded from screen. Several pieces of wire twisted together made the stem, which was wrapped with strips of green crepe paper. The leaves were attached as the stem was wrapped.

By the time spring arrived, we had packed several boxes of colorful paper flowers. Mother said I made excellent flowers, and year after year, we spent many happy hours working on them together.

In May, the excitement mounted. Dad scheduled his work around Memorial Day. The spring housecleaning was finished, and Mother planned menus, baked and cooked.

Mother tried to keep my excitement under control by keeping me busy helping her.

Vintage postcard, House of White Birches nostalgia archives

Aunts and uncles began to arrive. At first they traveled in wagons, and in later years, in automobiles. Each family arrived with food, bedding, decorations and children. There were plenty of hugs and kisses to go around. Everyone laughed and talked at once.

I had an aunt who was married to a doctor. They had more money than the others. She always brought a small gift for each of the children and a large bag of store-bought candy. How excited we were, waiting for their arrival! One year she brought each girl a necklace with a heart, and each boy a bag of marbles.

The women spent most of their time in the kitchen, preparing food and washing dishes. They laughed, talked, exchanged recipes and enjoyed it all. The men usually stayed outside under a shade tree. They talked, told jokes and kept their eyes on the multitude of children running around.

Although I enjoyed playing with my cousins, I also wanted to hear what the grown-ups were saying. I'd sneak into the kitchen and sit quietly, listening, until my mother spotted me. Outside I would go with a strong warning: "Children don't sit around and listen to adults talking. Children belong outside with the other children." I hated missing anything, but I knew better than to argue.

Long tables were set outside at mealtime. The abundance of mouth-watering food was memorable. Platters held everything from baked ham to golden-brown fried chicken.

The tables were also loaded with a variety of salads, baked beans, hot rolls, pies and cakes. Kool-Aid was our drink, with coffee and tea for the adults. Everyone ate until they couldn't hold another bite.

Since there were so many relatives, beds were made inside on the floor and outside on the lawn. At night, I enjoyed gathering all the children together and telling them scary stories. Sometimes I would have at least half of them crying. I'd get into trouble for that, but we had a lot of fun.

That night, after the chores were finished and everyone had eaten, Dad would build a large bonfire.

The day before Memorial Day was the day for decorating. Since the cemeteries weren't covered with grass as they are now, Dad let our grass grow long. The men would mow the lawn, sack the grass, cut fresh greenery and gather lavender lilacs. The women packed their paper flowers, found vases for the lilacs and gathered up the children.

At the cemetery, weeds were pulled and everything was raked and cleaned. Next, each grave was covered with fresh grass. Then the decorating would begin.

Stories were told about each loved one as we worked. There were tears and laughter. Children were encouraged to help so they could learn their families' histories. The decorating continued until every grave was a beautiful riot of color.

That night, after the chores were finished, and everyone had eaten, Dad would build a large bonfire. Chairs and logs were moved around the fire. An uncle who wrote and sold stories would read them to us. I was fascinated by them. Children roasted marshmallows, and the night air rang with merriment. As the children became sleepy, they were put to bed. I always tried to stay awake as long as the adults did, but I never did.

On Memorial Day, we would dress in our finery and return to the cemetery. Since almost everyone else in town would be there with their families, it was a time to see old friends. Many times, people were still milling around at sundown, visiting and admiring decorations.

In our family as in many others, this old-time tradition is mainly a thing of the past. That's sad, because our family gatherings created warm memories and kept us in touch with our roots.

Now, when I am walking through the cemetery, telling my children and grandchildren the history of family and friends, I find I know more people in the cemetery than I do people still living. I've wondered what that means. I've come to the conclusion I must be getting old. ❖

That's My Daddy

By Angie Monnens

I think about my daddy so often because he was interested in a variety of things—important things, like freedom, politics, prejudice, wars and any other happenings of yesterday, as well as those in the present time. He, of course, is no longer with us, but while he lived, there wasn't anyone as loving, kind and thoughtful as my daddy.

The Lord had blessed him with a brilliant mind, which made it easy for him to learn and remember everything he read or heard. He passed his knowledge on to his children, and though I am not even a bit as bright as he was, he taught me the important things in life!

Perhaps the times I cherished most with him—he was busy, raising eight children and caring for our grandpa, who made his home with us—were national holidays.

These included Decoration Day (now we observe it as Memorial Day), the Fourth of July and Veterans Day (formerly called Armistice Day). On these special occasions, I saw my daddy in another light; somehow that tough exterior melted just a bit when his staunch patriotism came to the fore.

Perhaps the times I cherished most with him were national holidays.

As a child, I helped Daddy set out flags in our yard on these holidays. We placed small flags in the ground all along the narrow sidewalk that led from the street to our front door. Then Daddy taped medium flags to the old wooden porch pillars and a huge one onto the big oak tree near the corner of the yard.

When we finished, I followed him into the bedroom, sat on his bed and watched as he changed from his work shirt into a freshly ironed white Sunday shirt. From the bureau drawer he took out his Legionnaire's cap, went to the mirror and placed it on his head. He adjusted it a few times to make sure it was set at just the right angle.

Oh, he was so handsome! I noticed he looked somber and a bit sad because he would take part in the services for all who had given their lives in the service of our country. He had told me this many times, and though I couldn't comprehend the full meaning of war, it made me feel closer to him.

I knew these days brought back terrible memories of battles fought during World War I, especially when he took a bullet in the upper chest. He was carrying a picture of the girl who would later be my mother in his upper pocket, and the photo plainly shows where the bullet hit.

He seldom talked about the war, but once, when we had company, he described the utter horror and devastation of human lives he witnessed.

Facing page: *We Must Remember* by John Slobodnik, © House of White Birches nostalgia archives

"As the mines exploded," he told them, "all around me, bodies of my buddies were ripped apart. Arms and legs flew high into the air, and the moaning and groaning sounds could be heard throughout the area. It was *hell*!"

My siblings and I overheard this tale when we listened through the heat register on the floor of our bedrooms upstairs. We never told Daddy that we had listened in; it would have made him sad to think he had given us such a complete picture of a battle. He wanted us to know only happy things, yet he made us aware that life combined the good with the bad.

Daddy had great respect and love for our country and the flag. He instilled in all of us a feeling of awe and reverence at the opportunity to live in a free nation. I will always remember seeing my daddy cry when he saluted the flag as it went by, or when the soulful *Taps* was played. To this day, I still share Daddy's feeling when I see our flag waving high in the breeze. But the most heart-wrenching sound to me is when the trumpet sounds *Taps* at funerals. It was played at my daddy's and also my husband's.

Just as Daddy taught me to cherish the freedom we have been given, so, too, have I passed it on to my children and grandchildren. Of all the blessings God has provided us, the privilege of living in America and being able to follow our own beliefs is the greatest by far! ❖

A Rose for Father's Day

By Evelyn Witter

A red rose in a man's lapel on Father's Day means a child has paid him tribute. This is perhaps the most recognizable tribute you can pay your father this Father's Day.

The idea of Father's Day came about one June morning in 1909 when Mrs. John Bruce Dodd of Spokane, Wash., thought about her father, William Smart, a Civil War veteran who raised six motherless children on a Washington farm. It was nearing his birthday.

Slowly an idea developed. Why not have a certain Sunday set aside to honor all fathers? This day would call attention to the important place of the father in the home.

Mrs. Dodd went first to her own minister with the idea. He suggested that they talk to the Spokane Ministerial Association. Mrs. Dodd also wrote to the Spokane Ministers Alliance. They favored the idea of honoring fathers.

When the Spokane Young Men's Christian Association put the Father's Day idea before the people in 1910, the city of Spokane set aside a day to honor fathers.

William Jennings Bryan, secretary of state, was one of the first officials to give public approval to Mrs. Dodd's idea when he said, "Too much emphasis cannot be placed upon the relation between parent and child."

The importance of Father's Day grew when President Wilson had a Father's Day button pressed in the White House in 1916. It was President Calvin Coolidge who recommended a national observance of Father's Day in 1924. Mrs. Dodd selected the rose as the official Father's Day flower.

Since 1966, Father's Day officially has been observed throughout the United States on the third Sunday in June. According to the National Father's Day Committee, it is suggested that you wear a white rose in remembrance on Father's Day or give a red rose to your father for a living tribute. ❖

Laurels for Father

By Loise Pinkerton Fritz

Laurels for Father!
So may it be
Till time blends
Into eternity.

The third Sunday in June has been set aside for the observance of Father's Day. On this day, we bestow laurels upon Dad in appreciation for all he has done for us. This particular day (as well as all others, I must confess), I go to my make-believe bookshelf and reach for my Book of Memories. As I leaf through it, I find many little "pig ears" on the corners of the pages. One page, however, seems to have a larger ear than all the rest. It's a page that tells a beautiful story, for it always brings to mind our Lord's words: "I was thirsty, and ye gave me drink." Let me share the story with you.

When I was a little girl, each night before the family went to bed, we children had to have a drink of water from the long-handled dipper that was kept in the old-fashioned water bucket that stood on the sink. After each of us had had a drink, Dad would take the little glass-bottomed lit kerosene lamp and set it in the hallway upstairs. With the wick turned low, there was always a dim light to keep the night from being so dark.

Needless to say, as soon as we got into bed, we began talking about the joys of the day. Soon the talking turned to soft giggling, then laughter, and then shouting from room to room. It was at this point that Dad would tell us to settle down, say our prayers and go to sleep.

Many, many nights, Dad's orders were followed time and again by four little voices saying, one after another, "I'm thirsty for a drink of water." I'm certain no one would understand why we needed another drink of water … no one except Dad. Without hesitation, he would go downstairs and bring us a drink of water. Then we were off to dreamland.

Dad has never made the headlines in any paper; neither has he realized any great accomplishments according to man's standards. However, I'm certain that in God's Book of Life, there is recorded behind Dad's name these words: "Inasmuch as ye have done it unto one of the least of these, my brethren, ye have done it unto me." ❖

Fly the Flag High!

By Bonnie Lee Wells

*H**mm,* I thought, noticing the red check beside June 14 on my calendar. What was that about? I did a mental check of family members' birthdays and anniversaries and drew a blank. Finally, I put on my spectacles and read the fine print: "June 14, Flag Day. U.S. Army founded (1775)." My face grew hot with shame. Imagine me, a patriot, forgetting about Flag Day!

Oh, I know you're sick and tired of holidays that cost you a bundle. Talk about commercialization! The way stores put out Christmas displays, for example … and before we've even celebrated Thanksgiving! And then come Valentine's Day, Easter, Mother's Day, Father's Day and even Children's Day. (I wonder who thought *that* one up? I mean, isn't *every* day Children's Day?)

But I say, "Hats off to Flag Day!" Listen, it doesn't cost us a penny: You invest in a flag, take good care of it, and from then on, your only investment is an emotional one.

> *" The Flag of the United States represents the living country and is considered as a living thing."*

You say you don't feel an emotional attachment to Old Glory? Well then, consider this: What if you had been born in another country—like Russia, for example? Anyway, come June 14, remember to hoist the flag high, and maybe even go so far as to salute it. Not only will you feel good about yourself, but trust me—you'll drive the dissidents crazy!

If you are anything like me, you've forgotten most of what you were supposed to have learned in school about the flag. So, allow me to refresh your memory. It seems that Army Regulation 260-10, dated Oct. 25, 1944, gives a comprehensive explanation governing the display of the flag. It declares "The Flag of the United States represents the living country and is considered as a living thing." *A living thing.* I like that.

Nowadays we must deal with the controversy that has developed as to when and where American citizens (schoolchildren, in particular) may salute the flag and recite the Pledge of Allegiance. How ironic that this is a debate about a document that was written on Sept. 8, 1892, as part of a Columbus Day celebration. At the time, its authorship was left anonymous. Consequently, it wasn't until after the death of employees Francis Bellamy and James Upham (whose families both claimed authorship) that the United Flag Association investigated and ultimately concluded that the honor of being recognized as author of the Pledge of Allegiance belonged to Bellamy.

As originally published, it read, "I pledge allegiance to my flag and to the republic for which it stands: one nation, indivisible, with liberty and justice for all." The words "under God" were added later.

It wasn't until the first national Flag Conference in Washington in June 1923 that the words "my flag" were replaced by "the flag of the United States." At the second conference, "of America" appeared.

On June 14, 1923, representatives from 68 patriotic organizations met in Washington to draft a nationwide code of flag etiquette that resulted in the Uniform Flag Law.

June 14 was officially declared Flag Day in the National Flag Day Bill signed by President Harry S. Truman on Aug. 3, 1949. Consequently, the flag is rooted deep within the history and heart of America and American citizens.

One of my favorite authors is Henry David Thoreau, and one of my favorite quotes is found in his book, *Walden*: "For every thousand hacking at the leaves of evil, there is one striking at the root."

Unfortunately, most of us do merely hack at the leaves of evil, even though we could accomplish more good if we would strike at its roots. How do we do that? A good place to start would be to speak out against those who deliberately dishonor the flag by burning and spitting on it; who would, if given half a chance, delete the words "under God" from the Pledge of Allegiance.

And another suggestion: Since it's our God-given right to fly the flag of the United States of America on our own property, why don't more of us do it? And I don't mean on patriotic holidays only. Instead, let's fly Old Glory every day. And hear ye, hear ye, all you fellow patriots: Let's fly it high! ❖

Stars and Stripes Forever

By Anita Hunter

"Listen to that piccolo solo!" "That music makes me glad to be an American." "I can see why John Philip Sousa is called 'The March King.'" The Fourth of July celebration in our small Iowa town meant a lively band concert in the city park. Feet kept time with the rhythm and beat of the music, and we clapped until our hands were sore. We three 9-year-old girls marched from one end of the block to the other, sidestepping our parents' blankets on the grass.

When a slower sentimental ballad was on the program, we slipped across the street to buy 5-cent chocolate ice-cream cones at Potter's Polar Pantry. But now it was time for the grand finale. While the band played *Stars and Stripes Forever*, fireworks burst overhead, Roman candles sizzled, and we waved sparklers like batons, directing the show.

The heady smell of burnt firecrackers lingered in the air as we headed toward the family car. At home in bed, with my two girlfriends sleeping over, we tried to hum the melodies we had heard and relive the magical evening.

Years later, after I had children of my own, we attended Fourth of July concerts and fireworks in El Segundo, Calif. The town was named "The Second" in Spanish because it was the second installation built in California by Standard Oil.

I remember the pungent odor of fireworks mingled with the sweet aroma of star jasmine growing in the park, and the salt air blowing in from the nearby ocean. In addition, there was the unmistakable smell of gases drifting over from the adjacent refinery.

We eagerly awaited the playing of *Stars and Stripes Forever*, for by now, it had become an Independence Day tradition. That piece and John Philip Sousa's *Semper Fidelis*, the United States Marine Corps anthem, are probably the best known of the composer's many marches.

When I recently met his nephew, Robert Sousa, I listened with great interest to the story of John Philip's road to fame. As a 6-year-old boy, he wanted to play the trumpet, but his father, a trombone player in the Marine Band, said, "That instrument is too noisy. When you practice, it will bother our apartment neighbors. I can practice at the base, but you can practice your violin lessons at home. You'll learn to read music and appreciate classical composers."

Finally, at age 13, John Philip was apprenticed to the Marine Corps Band, where he learned to play many instruments, including the trumpet. He later became bandmaster of the U.S. Marine Corps Band. After 12 years in that position, he resigned to form his own concert band to tour and bring his music to towns and cities all over the country.

I still get a thrill on the Fourth of July when my feet start keeping time to *Stars and Stripes Forever*. I cannot resist clapping to the music of a military concert band as memories carry me back to those patriotic performances in our little Midwestern town. ❖

The Fourth in the '40s

By Luella Tuma Mullins

*I*t was early on this particular Fourth of July morning. The family was dressed in their most comfortable summer clothes. It was important that we get to the fairgrounds early to select our shade tree for the day. We knew this was to be a long, hot day. The picnic baskets were packed with all the goodies we could muster—pies, cakes, sandwiches, watermelons, Kool-Aid, cookies, potato chips, crackers, cheese, peanut butter and such.

The red-checkered tablecloth was folded nicely. We took colorful quilts to sit on. There were lawn chairs for the older folks, but we teenagers preferred to sit on quilts spread on the ground.

Fourth of July was the biggest "to-do" of the year. The county fair was combined with the celebration, so it was really a big deal for everyone.

In our little Texas town, we went "all out" to have things right for the event. The fairgrounds were in top shape. The racetrack had been graded and was smooth. Concession stands were everywhere. We could get most anything we wanted to eat or drink from these stands: hot dogs, hamburgers, corn on the cob, sausage on a stick, Cokes, root beer, Pepsi Cola, strawberry and orange soda pop and all the others. There was freshly pulled taffy, cotton candy, popcorn and roasted peanuts. We could smell the hickory-smoked meat from the barbecue stands a mile away.

The celebration included a carnival too. We teenagers rode all the rides, pitched pennies for stuffed toys and took special interest in the dunking

"Three cheers for the Red, White and Blue"!

Vintage postcard, House of White Birches nostalgia archives

booth, where we could throw a baseball at the red target and dunk our teachers, officials and other big shots. All the kids laughed when we dunked these local "celebrities."

Almost every youngster in town had his silhouette cut from black construction paper by a fat lady who worked with the carnival. There were sideshows too. We knew that many of them were fakes, but we liked them anyway.

Since it was also a county fair, there was a section where the FFA boys brought their stock to be judged and a section for the 4-H club boys and girls to display their entries and also win ribbons.

Farmers and their wives brought their vegetables and fruits, canned jellies and beautiful flowers. The ladies showed off their embroidered dresser scarves, crocheted bedspreads and doilies.

There were cash prizes for the FFA cattle and poultry, but everything else competed for blue, red and white ribbons.

The horse races were the main event of the day. Everyone loved the horses. The owners brought them from all around. There were several categories to enter. I didn't know much about the categories, but I did love the races. During the 1940s, it was illegal to bet in Texas, but since everybody knew everybody, maybe a few dollars changed hands sometimes.

As for me, I was too busy showing off my Charlie. He was a sailor I had my eye on. Luckily, he had gotten his leave at just the right time that year, and it was my chance to show all the other girls my beau. He looked so fine in his white sailor uniform with the little white sailor cap pushed back on his head. I wore my crisp, white sundress so we would match. We were about the best-looking couple around.

It was one of the hottest Fourths of July that I could remember. No one complained, though;

The author and her Charlie.

the concession stands just sold more cold drinks. To demonstrate just how hot it really was, one of the men fried an egg on the hot street. Now *that* is hot!

Charlie and I and our friends returned to our picnic spot under the big shade tree several times during the day to drink ice-cold water and rest a bit on the quilts before going again. It was such fun for everyone— even though I was sporting a sun-blistered face and a new crop of freckles before the day's end.

A country-and-western band of local musicians was playing in the bandstand. It was good music. Our county was filled with German and Bohemian people, so you know it was good picking and singing. And Bob Wills' band was to play for the street dance. We couldn't wait!

The day was going fast— the horse races were over, and the ribbons had been awarded. Everyone was hot and tired but happy. The sun was setting. It wouldn't be long before the fireworks were set off and the street dance began.

We all went back to the big shade tree once more for a big slice of cold watermelon and a rest. The boys talked about funny things that had happened during the day as they drank strawberry sodas. Charlie got so tickled that, all of a sudden, he spurted a big mouthful of red soda pop right down the front of my white sundress. What a mess! Right then and there, I told him he would buy me a new dress. Everyone laughed.

But that Fourth of July turned out to be the very best day of all for me. Charlie asked me to marry him, and I did. Now, 50-some years have passed. Charlie is still paying for that ruined dress. He has bought me many, many new dresses since then. But I won the best prize of all—I won my Charlie. ❖

The Night John Whistled at Grandma

By Brenda J. Jackson

*M*y early childhood in a community in southern Missouri consisted of carefree, adventure-filled days. In the late 1940s, most small-town children had the run of the streets and only checked in with their mothers for meals and the mandatory one-hour rest after eating. Two of my uncles lived in California with their families, but they always found a way to make a yearly trip back home to visit their Missouri relatives. (My California cousins always referred to this as "the trip to Misery.") Some years they visited at Christmastime, but more often they traveled by car or train to stay for two weeks during the summer.

I always looked forward to my cousins' vacations. Our neighbor had a large house with enough room to accommodate one of my aunts and her family. That meant that for two weeks, I had playmates next door.

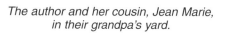

The author and her cousin, Jean Marie, in their grandpa's yard.

Cousin John was the "pain-in-the-neck" older brother to Jean Marie, who was my age. When John left us to play alone, Jean Marie and I got along quite well for two 6-year-olds from different parts of the country. But if he grew bored, he took delight in stirring up discontent between us. Cousin John seemed to know how to push all our buttons.

One year, my uncle earned the money for the trip home by operating a fireworks stand. Not only did he earn enough to drive his family to Missouri, but he brought along his unsold inventory. And so the Fourth of July 1949 was destined to be a holiday to remember.

It started normally. Back then, there were no laws regulating the use of firecrackers and other dangerous noisemakers, so our small town woke early to the sounds of penny packs of "ladyfingers" and the larger "cherry bombs." Boys raced about, searching for tin cans, old bottles and metal pipes to blow up. Large firecrackers placed under tin cans were exciting, but very hazardous. Bottle rockets whooshed skyward, ending with a *thock*!

Dogs cowered under their porches, fearing the *snap-snap-snap-snap*! when entire packages of small firecrackers suspended from clotheslines were lit. And the cows pastured in fields at the edge of town found more interesting grazing near the far fences on that day.

When Jean Marie and I tired of helping John find things to blow up, we contented ourselves by burning a few "snakes." We were timid about anything that had a fuse and made a loud bang.

John had a large supply of "whistlers," which consisted of a pinwheel with three little gizmos that blew sparks. We stood well back as he carefully placed one on a rock and lit the fuse. Then we all ran like crazy. The spinning pinwheel skipped along unpredictably, emitting an earsplitting whistle until the powder fizzled out. All kids loved whistlers.

Some time around noon, everyone piled into cars and met up at Grandpa's farm. There the families separated into three groups until supper. All the cousins ran to the barn to play in the hayloft. We also played in and around the farmhouse, generally getting in everyone's way.

Uncle Almon "Chub" Prater is pictured with the author's Aunt Halene, and cousins John and Jean Marie.

Mom and my aunts spent the afternoon in the large farm kitchen. Grandma ruled over the food preparations, but her daughters-in-law helped when they could. The menu, planned with a hot day in mind, consisted of many dishes that had been cooked in advance. After adding their contributions to the bowls on the large table, the women sat in straight-backed chairs pushed against the walls. As they talked about kids and friends, Grandma's smile was testament to how much she loved having everyone home.

Grandpa reigned over the front yard from his favorite chair on the porch. The other men stood, hunkered or leaned against porch posts near him. Their discussions tended to focus on crops, work, politics and the latest cars. We cousins all loved Grandpa very much because he took time for each of us. He always stopped to listen when a child came to tell him a story or ask an important question. We believed Grandpa knew the answer to everything! I learned in later years that if he didn't have the answer, he made one up. Whatever the case, the child left his porch happy.

After the evening meal, the men returned to the front yard while the women helped Grandma return order to the kitchen. We kids chased fireflies and burned sparklers while Grandpa directed the men to carry the kitchen chairs to the front yard. Then Grandma, my mother and all my aunts joined the group to sit with the men and talk as they watched us play with the last of the "safe" fireworks.

After all the firecrackers and snakes were depleted and the sparklers ran out, we kids began begging the men to start the show. My dad and uncles were in charge of setting off the large fireworks. First, the Roman candles were lit, one at a time. Each child was allowed to hold one under close supervision. We were cautioned over and over to always hold the candle out from our bodies and point it away from the family. Each bright ball of color erupting from the cardboard cylinder was met with "oohs!" and "aahs!" from our mothers.

Next came the cones, spewing fountains of sparks and flames in assorted colors. These brought even more exclamations of admiration.

At this point, we kids were directed to sit on quilts on the ground while the men set off the large, dangerous skyrockets. Some distance from the house, a large piece of pipe wedged between rocks was used to direct the large rockets. Each burst in the dark sky was spectacular.

When the last was fired, the show came to an end. We sleepy children, too tired to play anymore, lay listening to the adults talk.

Grandpa asked John to take a paper bag and pick up the trash left around the porch and yard. I watched as my cousin grabbed a sack and strutted off with an air of importance. First he scoured the yard near the house. Then he went out to the pipe to pick up the trash there. As he picked up a sack, I noticed that he first shook it and then paused to look inside.

I elbowed Jean Marie in the ribs and pointed at her brother. He walked to the pile of rocks, removed the pipe and laid it to one side. Then he reached into the bag and pulled something out.

Only then did I realize that he had found one last whistler. Without apparent thought to the consequences, he placed the pinwheel on a flat rock and lit the fuse. He quickly backed away. A piercing whistle and shower of sparks shattered the night's peace. Then the whistler took off, headed straight for Grandma and the women. They squealed and scrambled to get out of its path, but as Grandma struggled to rise, her chair tipped over backward and her feet flew over her head.

Fortunately, no real harm was done. After helping Grandma up, everyone turned to find John standing with his hands over his mouth, his eyes large and shining in the reflected light from the house. Grandpa broke the stunned silence first with a half-suppressed sputter, then a chuckle, and finally, a deep, rumbling laugh. When Grandma joined in, so did everyone else.

Grandpa was laughing so hard that tears streamed down his face. "Boy," he said, wiping his wet cheeks, "you sure know how to end a fireworks show!" ❖

A Big Boom

By Ethel Weehunt

At our house, the Fourth of July was a day of celebration. Early in the morning, Mama hung the red, white and blue flag on a porch post.

Papa solemnly said the Pledge of Allegiance as my sister, brother and I, hands over our hearts, joined in: "I pledge allegiance to the flag of the United States of America, and to the Republic for which it stands; one nation indivisible, with Liberty and Justice for all." (We didn't say "under God" as those words were not added to the pledge until 1954.)

During my childhood, Okemah, Okla., did not sell fireworks, but nearby Castle did. Before Independence Day, Mama drove us to Castle to buy them.

Mama cooked up a sure-enough American noon dinner while we froze the ice cream to go with the chocolate cake that would follow the fried chicken and garden vegetables.

Our horde of fireworks waited on the porch for darkness to arrive. Finally it did.

First, we fired the loud *boom-bang* firecrackers, which made Duke, our dog, head for the barn. "Let him in the house," Mama said sympathetically. "The noise hurts his ears." Then came colorful Roman candles, and last, the starry sparklers and scary snakes-in-the-grass.

The final show was hard to believe. Papa, enthused by the lights, the happy shouts and patriotic Fourth of July spirit, stuffed a 5-foot-long, 1-inch-wide pipe with gunpowder. He rammed the powder down against a rag, dropped a heavily oiled string to reach the gunpowder, struck a match to the string, and ran, yelling, "Get back! Get way back!"

Did we have a boom? Yes, we had a *terrific* boom that split the pipe and lit the whole yard. Cowering behind Mama on the porch, we heard her admonish Papa, "Now, that'll do for this year."

All of us remember the Fourth of July when Papa split the pipe. ❖

A Boy, a Dog and a Race

By Kyle F. Waite
As told to Shirley Pope Waite

The Fourth of July dawned clear and warm in Twin Falls, Idaho, in 1929. It promised to be another great holiday, a celebration filled with activities, concession stands all over town, races and other contests for young and old alike. Some events were even for mixed groups.

The activity that interested me was the first-ever boy-and-dog race. This particular race would be run in accordance to three specific rules:

1) The boy had to be 11 or 12 years old;

2) The dog must constantly be on a leash; and

3) The boy and dog had to cross the finish line at the same time.

The notice for this event was published about two weeks before the Fourth by the Ford Motor Co. so that entrants could have some practice time. The prize was a 1925 Model-T Ford touring car.

Author Kyle Waite at age 11 with his dog, Freckles, and a pet lamb.

My dog was a Boston screwtail bulldog, quite small but very compact. Freckles and I began our workouts. I started our practices by teaching Freckles not to jump the gun or start early. We would then trot slowly through the length of the race. This was to teach the dog to stay close to me and run at my speed.

Then an unusual thing happened. A pet lamb we owned started showing interest in our daily race and began to run with us. By race day, the three of us had the details down pat.

During practice sessions, we drew quite a crowd of neighbors to watch.

Then came the big day! To an 11-year-old boy, it seemed like everyone in the county was on hand to see the big race. What an uproar! Just imagine all the strange dogs coming together in one place. Dogfights were going on all over the street. Kids were screaming at their dogs and at each other. But my little bulldog and I just stood there and watched. (The little lamb was left at home.)

The officials finally got things quieted down and prepared to start the big event. The course would cover two blocks down Shoshone Street and back to Main. All the boys and their dogs lined up across Main Street. The gun fired, and the race was on!

The firing of the starting gun got the dogs excited again, but Freckles and I ran just as we had practiced. Dogs were running wild all around us. Some boys fell down, while others were dragged by their big animals. It was quite a mess.

Needless to say, Freckles and I crossed the winner's line first, and for our efforts, we won the 1925 Model-T Ford touring car. Of course, I couldn't drive, so an older friend of the family took over during the summer months.

The fun was rather short-lived, but that fall I sold the car for enough to buy a used cornet so I could begin music lessons.

Because I was still under 12 years of age that next Fourth of July, I was eligible to compete in the race again. And I won a second car, a 1926 Model-T Ford coupe. This meant extra money for school expenses, which helped my folks during those early Depression days. ❖

July Fourth, 1935

By Charley Sampsell

When June arrived in 1935, I began to watch for the mailman, Bob Maher, with increasing impatience each day. It was time to receive my copy of the annual catalog from Spencer Fireworks Co. in Polk, Ohio. To an 11-year-old farm boy of Mendon, Mich., the Spencer catalog was a combination wish book and scientific journal.

Each year, the seemingly myriad selection of firecrackers—ranging from tiny ladyfingers to bombs the size of sticks of dynamite—was more exciting. There were also many new models of cap guns, skyrockets, smoke bombs and novelties to study carefully to avoid a mistake in committing one's entire holiday budget.

As soon as the magical book arrived, it took me about a week of concentrated study to select a dozen different packs of firecrackers, a new cap gun and a generous supply of caps. I knew that before I stamped my order and took the letter down to the mailbox, I could expect my dad to stroll by, look over my shoulder and ask, "What are you ordering there, Cappy?"

The author and his mother, Kleo, in 1935.

That was a prelude to his telling me he would favor me by ordering a few additional items so that Spencer's would give my trade more serious consideration. Even I could see right through that ruse. He really needed a dozen or so of the biggest firecrackers they sold. Those beauties looked about a foot long and a couple of inches in diameter, just slightly larger than a stick of dynamite.

After mailing my order to Spencer's, another period of intense waiting began. Since fireworks could not be mailed, our shipment had to come by railway express to Mendon, about 5 miles from our farm. The Mendon railway express agent, who was also the depot manager, ticket seller, baggage handler and janitor, would mail us a postcard to notify us to pick up the package. Once again, the mailman's arrival was the highlight of my day.

After about a week, the suspense was unbearable, and my dad, with apparent reluctance, consented to make our weekly trip to town a couple of days early. So, after finishing the chores the next morning, my mom, my dad and I all piled into our good old black 1928 four-door Buick sedan and chugged away toward Mendon.

There were a couple of straight stretches on our route where Dad actually got the speedometer needle up over 35 miles an hour, hinting at his own enthusiasm and causing my mother to exclaim, "Charley, slow down!"

When we got there, the express agent gave us the unwelcome news that our package had not yet arrived, but the morning train had not yet pulled in. We did some shopping at Riley's Grocery and Shoemaker's Hardware, always listening intently for the train whistle.

Finally, we heard it, and I led the charge back to the Buick. Dad burned as much rubber as a 1928 model could on our return to the depot.

God answers all prayers, even though sometimes the answer is "No." On that day, the answer was "Yes," and there was our glorious 3-foot box from Spencer Fireworks. There are few experiences more fun than opening that kind of package. It was one of my best days.

Dad had ordered six skyrockets with long sticks. I began using my fireworks immediately, with good intentions of saving half for the Fourth of July. But Dad squirreled away his order for use only on the holiday.

My cap guns were essential to any pretense of being Buck Jones or Ken Maynard, and thus were used daily. During the latter part of June, I employed my firecrackers chiefly in the name of scientific experimentation. I conducted a study on how high a tin can would rise when propelled by one or more explosive charges. I also probed the effects of igniting buried propellants on compacted dirt and other natural and manmade materials.

Finally the Fourth of July arrived, finding me with slightly less than half of my supplies remaining. I began firing in earnest after breakfast, working with one smoldering punk after another.

At about 10 a.m., I was getting ready to simultaneously light three crackers in a drainpipe. As I bent over to apply my lighting punk to the fuses, the world suddenly exploded in an ear-blasting cloud of frightening sound. Involuntarily, I leaped away from my work and stood there, shaking, for several seconds before I realized that Dad had fired his first shot of the day out in back of the barn about 30 yards away. For the rest of the day, that happened intermittently, but only when least expected. My dad didn't mind others enjoying the sound of his jumbo crackers, but he wanted to fire them alone. But I knew he would share his skyrockets with me when night fell.

While we were eating lunch (we called it "dinner" in those days) at the kitchen table, Mom asked Dad, "Charley, are you going to keep on playing with your fireworks out there in back of the barn all day? You had better watch out you don't set the straw stack on fire!"

Dad just smiled and said, "Don't worry about it." He was always a man of few words and didn't like lengthy debates.

The afternoon progressed nicely with frequent detonations from all points around the house and barnyard. Later, Mom had Dad hitch old Tom, one of our two workhorses, to the buggy so that she could drive to her best friend Linna's house for a visit. With nobody left to complain about our celebration, Dad and I accelerated our activities.

Late in the afternoon, I began to get hungry and went to the front yard to watch for Mom to return. As she rounded Ernst's Corner about a quarter-mile from our house, I ran down our 100-yard driveway to the road and climbed into the buggy with her as she turned into the drive. Old Tom picked up his pace, perhaps thinking of the pan of oats he would get when Dad let him into his stall.

Mom had been born and raised on a farm, and she could drive a horse or team like a pro. She pulled into the dusty barnyard and backed the buggy up to the shed under the haymow in the barn.

"Whoa, Tom, back, haw, haw," she said. Tom turned to the left and backed the buggy cleanly into the shed until it touched the back wall of the barn.

Then it happened. Dad had been sitting out in back of the barn on the water tank by the pump, enjoying a pipe full of Union Leader, when he felt the urge to torch another of his sticks of dynamite. He lit it calmly and threw it safely away from him toward the barn. The

shocking report caused old Tom to lunge forward out of the shed, across the barnyard, through the gate, past the pine trees beside the house and down the driveway.

Mom lost her balance when the blast sounded and dropped the reins to grab the buggy seat. While she struggled to regain the seat, I was on the floor of the buggy, desperately trying to grab the reins, which had caught on the whip holder.

We had about 10 yards to go before we reached the road—and a certain upset if we rounded the corner at that speed—when Mom

The author's dad, Charley Sr., and cousin, Kenneth Brown, with old Tom hitched to the buggy.

regained control, sawed on the reins and screamed, "Whoa, Tom, whoa!" Tom dug in his heels and stopped immediately.

When we had regained our composure, Mom turned the buggy around, and we headed back up the drive. Dad met us at the barnyard gate, saying, "I wonder why that fool horse went crazy and ran away like that?"

There were no harsh words exchanged in my presence, but both my parents were unusually quiet for the rest of the holiday. When Dad and I were shooting off his skyrockets that night, he made me be extra careful to aim them all as far away from the house as possible. It was a very memorable Fourth of July for me in 1935.

In June 1936, when the Spencer catalog came, Dad increased his order for giant firecrackers from 12 to 18. That was another good year. ❖

The Cannon

By Violet Capizzi

Not many people have a cannon in their basement, but we did. My father built a small cannon with big wheels and a barrel about 2 feet long, and he painted it bright green. It was brought out of the basement only on the Fourth of July.

That cannon was my father's pride and joy. He would load it with paper wadding and the necessary gunpowder. When it was fired, it shot paper all over the lawn and produced a very loud *kaboom*!

He would shoot it off on the Fourth of July as his way of celebrating the holiday. Most of the men and the children in the neighborhood looked forward to this special celebration too.

But the next day, we children would have to gather up the bits of paper and put them in the trash barrel. We didn't mind when we were small, but as we grew older, we were not too happy about this cleanup job.

My mother didn't like *anything* about the cannon. She did her best to talk my father into getting rid of it.

He had several offers from his fellow sportsmen to buy it, but he refused to part with it.

As the years passed, he didn't fire it every year. But when World War II came along and I was an Army nurse stationed overseas, he vowed he would shoot it off the day the war was over, and I was on my way home.

So it was that on V-Day, he and many of our neighbors went out to hear the little cannon's victory *kaboom*! My friends and even my mother wrote to tell me about the cannon's salute to victory.

Some years went by before the cannon was fired again. That last time was when my children were old enough to celebrate Independence Day. My father fired it that morning. Then he solemnly announced that this was the last time it would be fired. The next day, he gave it to a local veterans' organization. Its silence would be a symbol of the peace we hoped had come to stay. ❖

My Skyrocket Ride

By Robert Longfellow

The year was 1931 and it was the Fourth of July. I was 12 years old, and my brother Jack was 15—the same age as our Uncle Gill, who was joining us for a day of youthful fun. Our 1929 Oldsmobile kicked up lots of dust as we headed for the old settlers' grounds in northern Kansas, just a short distance from the Nebraska border. For special celebrations and holidays, the old settlers who had homesteaded in that part of the state had built a large, barn-like building. It was surrounded by big black walnut trees and acres of gooseberry bushes—a perfect setting.

The building had a rough-hewn plank floor and a small step-up stage where local musicians played for dancing. The musicians, all volunteer farm folk, included many fiddlers, a lady harmonica player, guitarists galore and one old whiskered gent who could really get with it on a slide trombone. (He used to sell an all-purpose elixir from his wagon before he settled down to farming. It was local gossip that the sheriff had lots to do with him changing occupations.)

For weeks after that, I flew in my dreams every night.

Dirt roads coming in from all angles brought many farmers and friends to celebrate the Fourth of July. Wagons by the dozen, spring buggies, classy, fringed-top dandies and even a manure spreader with makeshift seats brought friendly groups of celebrants.

I can still see the many automobiles haphazardly parked all over the place: Ford T's, Model A's, a couple of roadsters with the tops down. Our neighbor Cecil and his 11 kids pulled up alongside our car in their Pierce Arrow touring sedan. Dad laughed; he said old Cecil had so many kids, it took a big boat to get 'em all in one place.

To start the Fourth of July celebration, it was customary for the original old-timers to ignite the "anvil bomb." Far from the crowd, a very large anvil was hauled up and placed on a knoll. Dad said they would pack it with black powder and set it off with a fuse.

We watched the man light the fuse, then run as if the devil were chasing him. In a few moments, there was an ear-splitting *boom!* and, in a cloud of smoke, the big anvil lifted straight up, then crashed to earth. Everyone whooped and hollered. The celebration of the Fourth had officially started.

Tables groaned with food. Kids competed in the sack race (in which I finished last). There was a pie-eating contest and a three-legged race that was fun, especially with my favorite girlfriend. The afternoon was filled with firecrackers popping off every second and kids squirting watermelon seeds at each other. Mother had packed a bunch of sandwiches and fruit for lunch.

A store owner from Superior, Neb., had driven the short distance and set up a cold-drink stand. He sold grape Nehi soda pop for 7 cents a bottle from a No. 3 washtub full of block ice.

He kept his business coming back as he would refund 1 cent if the buyer returned the empty bottle. We kids all agreed he was going home a rich man.

We had been given 50 cents each from Mother's egg money, and we invested the combined money in a huge bag of fireworks. The afternoon was quickly going by, our fireworks were dwindling down to a few sidewalk sulfur snakes, and I was mad because I stuck a lighted firecracker into the barrel of my prized cap pistol. When it exploded, the barrel flew apart in three pieces, ruining my gun and my day.

Dad said it was about time we gathered up our stuff and started for home. At that precise moment, we all heard a roar coming from the sky. Spellbound, we stood and watched a bright yellow bi-wing airplane swoop low over our heads, the pilot waving. I had never seen a real airplane before, and was I thrilled by the noise and confusion it caused. Dad said it was a barnstormer who usually followed special events and charged people money to fly with him.

The pilot skillfully landed the biplane on a strip of dirt road. When he came to a stop just a short distance from us, the wood propeller ceased its revolutions. Painted in red on both sides of the plane was the word *Skyrocket*. With something other than a graceful leap from the cockpit, the man landed on his feet and said, "Hello."

I remember in detail how exciting he looked in his leather cap with flapping earmuffs. His big goggles were propped above his eyebrows and his leggings were laced up to his knees.

He charged $2 a trip. After much begging and pleading by all of us kids, my folks finally said we could take a ride with him. Reluctantly, Mother dug into her egg money again.

When it was my turn, the pilot tossed me into what he called a cockpit. I was instructed to be sure the belt webbing around my waist remained snapped into the clip.

He really scared me when he said if we did a loop-de-loop he wouldn't want me to fall out!

Right then and there, I was ready to get out, but he revved the engine, and we were racing down the dirt road. Just as it appeared we would smash into a clump of trees, he pulled it up and we skimmed over the treetops. Clutching the sides of the cockpit, I hung on for dear life.

The pilot took a bottle out of his jacket and swigged for a long while. I just assumed he was taking medicine for a sore throat or something, and I could've cared less when I found out my cheeks would blow out when I opened my mouth.

Looking down at the tiny people and treetops way below me, I prayed the floor slats under my seat would stop vibrating. I could just see the floor opening, and me and the seat cushion falling to earth.

We circled the grounds endlessly—or so it seemed to me. When we came in for the landing, we clipped a few twigs off the trees with the wheels before we hit the road with a series of hard bumps. As we rolled to a stop, I was thankful it was over. I never admitted it to anyone, but I had the dickens scared out of me.

We left for home and arrived in time to do the chores. While I was milking our old cow, my head comfortably resting on the side of Bossy's large bag, my thoughts were high in the sky. For weeks after that, I flew in my dreams every night.

Now, many years later, I board a luxury sky monster, settle down in a comfortable seat and recall a memory: when my guardian angel and I soared into my first flight in a canvas-covered, wooden-frame, glued-and-wired-together biplane piloted by a happy drunk! ❖

My Most Memorable Fourth of July

By David B. Smith

During the 1930s, I grew up in the village of Mexico, N.Y., near Syracuse. My father, Charles T. Smith, was principal of the public school, and my mother, Elsie, was in full charge of housekeeping, bill paying and serving as the family heart-warmer. My older sister and brother, Evelyn and Charles L., were in high school.

Back then, our fun varied with the time of year. Each season had its own special games, pastimes and holidays. Fall was great for touch football and Halloween. Winter was Christmas and ice-skating. Spring beckoned with sap from our maple tree, softball and Easter.

But it was summer vacation that really put joy into our hearts! Not only was school out, but we could drive to the beach, partici-

pate in picnics, go to evening band concerts in Syracuse and Ohio, and celebrate the Fourth of July! Life couldn't get any better than this!

Next to Christmas, the Fourth of July was my favorite holiday. My most memorable Fourth was in 1940, when I was 8 years old. School was over by the last week in June, so my playmate Jeanette Robinson and I planned and performed a circus to raise money for fireworks. We sang songs, performed daring stunts on the lower limbs of my backyard butternut tree, told all the latest knock-knock jokes and displayed fantastic tricks by "my" dog Sandy. She could do "roll over," "speak" and "say your prayers," among other things. We charged 2 cents admission and made a wee bit of pocket change.

As always, our family had received catalogs from two mail-order fireworks companies. Fireworks were legal then in New York state. One company had lower prices but charged for postage. The other charged slightly more for their items but sent them postpaid.

Decisions, decisions! How we would pore over the offerings of cherry bombs, ladyfingers, Roman candles, pinwheels, skyrockets, volcanoes, caps and sparklers! We would read and reread the descriptions and prices, trying to get the most bang for the buck, quite literally.

The big day finally arrived, and I got up early. I was allowed to set off the little ladyfinger crackers, as they were considered relatively safe. The bigger boys in the neighborhood put cherry bombs under tin cans and blew them sky high!

The daytime fireworks quickly went up in smoke. Then there was nothing much to do but wait for the parade. A few of us boys decided to play war with rubber-band guns while the girls played hopscotch.

We made the guns ourselves from two sticks of wood, two nails and several rubber strips, or bands, cut from old inner tubes begged from the garage. When the handle was squeezed, the rubber strip flew off at terrific speed. If you got touched by one, you were out of the game.

It was nearly 11 o'clock when we finally walked downtown for the parade. We were all given American flags (with 48 stars back then). The floats had taken several weeks to prepare, and they were a sight to see, as were the fire engines, marching bands, the groups from lodges, clubs and schools, and the military units. It certainly was a grand, once-a-year event!

Vintage postcard, House of White Birches nostalgia archives

After the parade, my friends and I bought an ice-cream cone. John Shumway's dad ran the drugstore that had the ice-cream counter. The cones were a nickel, any flavor. Anyone who was rich enough to have 10 cents could buy an ice-cream soda. But 10 cents was also the price for admission to the Saturday afternoon movies at the town hall, so we seldom bought sodas!

In the afternoon, Dad drove us to the beach near Selkirk Shores on Lake Ontario. We had a small cabin there (it had started out as Dad's pigeon coop until Mom got a better idea). I always bought a pair of Sugar Daddy candy bars from the beach candy wagon. You got two for a nickel instead of one of anything else.

We drove home, and after supper, we listened to *Jack Armstrong, the All American Boy* on the radio and then went out to play a game of Kick the Can. When it began to get dark, we went over to my grandparents' house so they could watch us shoot off our fireworks. Sis liked the pinwheels that we always hung and ignited on Gram's catalpa tree.

Time has passed on. We have not lived in Mexico for over 50 years. Sandy sleeps eternally beneath that butternut tree. The maple tree, demolished by lightning, has long since fueled someone's fireplace. Car tires no longer use inner tubes. Fireworks are sadly illegal.

In 1977, my dad died at Plattsburgh, N.Y.— on July 4. The Fourth of July will always have special memories for me. ❖

Knights of Labor Holiday

By Juddi Morris

September is National Sewing Month, National Honey Month, National Chicken Month, National Piano Month and National Chile Month. But the holiday we celebrate on the first Monday in September is unique. It's the day our country has set aside to honor the very backbone of our nation—its workforce. Imagine, a day of rest and play that celebrates work!

The summer is almost over, school is starting and autumn colors are just over the horizon. The exodus starts toward mountains, lakes, beaches and one last visit to Grandma's before school starts.

Labor Day is 126 years old. In the beginning, it was not celebrated all over the nation—only in New York City. As early as 1882, the city had thousands of workers, and as a rule, their workday stretched from 12 to 14 hours, six or seven days a week. Overtime pay was unheard of. Adults were paid so little that for families to survive, children had to join the workforce.

Boys of 11 or 12 were already shoveling coal in the mines, working 10 hours a day in factories or lifting rolls of carpet. Small bodies toiled in sweatshops, and parents ached to see their children bent and stooped from hard labor.

Workers were helpless to change conditions until the 1880s, when they began to form craft unions under the umbrella of the Knights of Labor. They set out to get children out of the factories and mines; they fought for better pay, shorter hours and safer working conditions.

Many of these laborers were immigrants who came from countries where workers had been recognized with special holidays including picnics and parades. But such was not the case in their new country. The United States had no holiday to honor its labor force.

A smaller group, a part of the Knights of Labor called the Central Labor Union, decided to hold a labor festival in New York City. A carpenter named Peter McGuire is credited with ramrodding that first celebration.

It was decided to celebrate in September, as the first proclamation said, "It would come at the most pleasant season of the year, nearly midway between the Fourth of July and Thanksgiving, and would fill a wide gap in the chronology of legal holidays."

A grand parade was held with each craft union taking part. The jewelers' and bricklayers' unions furnished brass bands. Following the musicians were horse-drawn wagons, floats, horses and walkers holding banners touting their craft or work group. Before the parade ended that day, 10,000 workers marched down Fifth Avenue. Traffic stopped as thousands of people crowded the street to watch, cheer and wave handkerchiefs at the marchers.

On Monday, Sept. 5, 1882, Labor Day was born.

After the parade, a huge picnic was held at Elm Park. Fifty thousand people brought lunches and enjoyed a warm September afternoon. Fireworks that evening ended the wonderful day.

And so, on Monday, Sept. 5, 1882, Labor Day was born. It was so successful that another was held the next year, and the next. Five years later, Oregon became the first state to legalize Labor Day as a state holiday. Massachusetts, New Jersey, Colorado and New York quickly passed similar laws. Soon 23 states had established Labor Day observances. Congress jumped on the bandwagon and passed legislation making it a legal holiday in 1894.

Labor Day has undergone many changes through the years. In the beginning, parades, festivals and picnics were held. But now the holiday has encompassed not only the laboring class, but professionals also.

Still, it's a day to remember that all workers are important, no matter what job they hold. ❖

An Important Day

*By Olive Workman Persinger
as told to Donna McGuire Tanner*

It does not seem to be as important as it was in days gone by, but in my yesterdays, Labor Day was a grand time of celebration. This was during a time when most men in the labor force in West Virginia were coal miners. Labor Day was a gathering event for most of the men and their families. Every year, a convention was held in Beckley or Montgomery, W.Va.

In 1948, Montgomery hosted the annual event. It was to be a special day; my husband, Melvin Myers, and our daughter, Linda (not yet 3 years old), and I joined my sister Rachel, her husband, Basil, their son, Danny (almost 4 years old), their baby, Donna, and Basil's teenage brother, Clinton, at the celebration.

There was so much entertainment and music going on that it was hard to decide what to do first. There were concession stands and vendors everywhere. We bought cotton candy, hot dogs and barbecue sandwiches.

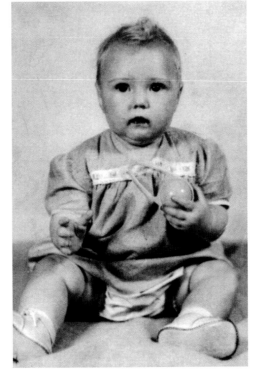

*Donna June McGuire, the author's niece,
Labor Day 1948.*

Even though World War II had ended three years earlier, some products still were in short supply. When we learned by word of mouth that there were laundry-soap chips for sale, all of us bought a huge supply—even Clinton, to take to his mother.

This was in the days before folding baby strollers, or strollers for rent, so we took turns carrying baby Donna. Her Uncle Clinton was toting her when we all stopped to let a photographer take her picture.

While the photographer was setting up for the picture, his assistant asked, "What do you feed this healthy child?"

In all seriousness, Donna's Uncle Clinton replied, "Buttermilk and corn bread."

The girl believed him, and then she remarked, "She sure does look like her father." We all laughed.

Later, when Donna's parents picked up the photo, they noticed that the pink dress she had been wearing was blue in the picture. The photographer explained that he had it colored that way to match her eyes.

After the visit with the photographer, it was on to the more serious side of the day. Many people made speeches, and we listened to most of them. But the entire large crowd had come to hear one speaker in particular: John L. Lewis, president of the United Mine Workers. Most miners thought he was a man to be admired.

Finally night fell. All the speeches were finished, and all the food had been devoured. Then all eyes turned toward the black sky to watch the spectacular fireworks.

Those fireworks were unlike any we had ever seen—real works of art. I remember the American flag in all its glory, President Harry Truman's face beaming down at us, and even the White House, blazing bright, lighting up the West Virginia heavens. It was indeed a prideful American display.

I have never forgotten Labor Day 1948. It was an important day. ❖

Autumn Treats

Chapter Three

My favorite memories of autumn holiday treats didn't come at Halloween, as it did for a lot of kids back in the Good Old Days. I have to say that the highlight of the fall holidays was Thanksgiving, the day we went to Grandpa and Grandma Tate's.

Grandpa and Grandma Tate had 13 children and raised 11 of them to adulthood. Thanksgiving was the holiday when those children and their progeny—usually numbering over a hundred—came to pay honor to Grandpa and Grandma.

Our Thanksgiving traditions at Grandpa and Grandma Tate's were not like the traditions of today. There were too many of us to in turn recite what we were thankful for. Our traditions were very basic and simple. We drove the few miles, singing "Over the river and through the woods …" all the way to my grandparents' home.

Then my brother, sister and I joined the melee of our cousins and second cousins while Daddy and Mama went inside carrying our share of the feast. All of the youngsters were relegated to the out-of-doors. There were far too many of us to fit inside the small house, a simple four-room home.

So whether it was playing, resting or eating, it was done outside. The "necessary room" was also out-of-doors, so that part of business was conducted outside as well. I'm thankful there were not too many rainy, cold Thanksgiving Days in those Ozark Mountains.

The women and older girls pulled the Thanksgiving dinner together. The men whittled and jawed. A few pitched horseshoes one last time before the quickly approaching winter.

Then it was time. The adults flowed to the front porch, calling to the youngsters who then swarmed like ants to the front yard. Then, on cue it seemed, we bowed our heads as Grandpa nodded to one of his sons to ask a blessing on the food.

As we stood in that front yard of the old farmhouse, heads bowed, I think there was a connection that transcended the four generations that were gathered. Caught in that brief glow of Thanksgiving tradition, we were all one.

One tradition from Thanksgiving dinner was that two of us children were chosen to pull the wishbone—that special bone from the breast of the turkey. We always looked forward to that and excitedly anticipated who would be selected for the honor.

The one who got the short part of the wishbone would be granted a wish.

The one who got the short part of the wishbone was assured that his or her wish would be granted in the next year. But the wishbone was a double-edged sword; the one left with the longer part of the bone had to help with dishes.

After dinner, the play was a little more subdued, the talk perhaps a little more philosophical. By the time the day was spent, so were we. The long shadows from the towering oaks in the front yard told us another Thanksgiving Day was over. Another round of hugs for Grandma, a few hasty goodbyes to favorite cousins, and we were on our way home again.

Thanksgiving was the crown jewel of the autumn holidays, a time to reflect on the fullness of the year quickly fading. Even in the toughest of times, our cups ran over with the most important elements: laughter and love, faith and family.

Innocently, I thought it would be like that forever. In some ways I guess it is; the faces have just changed and are fewer every year. I have so much to be thankful for each year as Thanksgiving approaches. Still, I miss the years when we were numbered by the scores instead of the ones—the Thanksgivings of the Good Old Days.

—Ken Tate

Facing page: *Sharing a Thanksgiving Wish* by John Slobodnik, © House of White Birches nostalgia archives

All Hallow's E'en

By Selma McCarthy

*I*t was Halloween 1931, and I was really excited! My best friend, Darlene, had invited me to eat supper, spend the night, and go with her and her mother to the Halloween parade. I could hardly wait! When Mr. Welton rang the 4 o'clock dismissal bell at Tecumseh Grade School, Darlene and I shot out of school like two cannonballs—after an orderly march down the hall, of course. Miss Wickwire, the first-grade teacher (I loved her), always played *March of the Wooden Soldiers* on the hall piano at recess and at dismissal time.

We ran most of the eight blocks home. In those days, only children who lived in rural areas had school-bus services. We didn't qualify. When we were within a block of home (we lived next door to each other), we could smell the yeast rolls that Darlene's mother was famous for baking. Everyone in our neighborhood loved them, especially me.

The parade started, led by a red devil carrying his long pointed tail.

Mrs. Dutton had invited my mother over for supper too. Great day!

When we got home, Mother and Mrs. Dutton were dipping up homemade vegetable soup for all of us. Coupled with the hot rolls, the soup made a wonderful supper. Mrs. Dutton was probably the best cook in town, and we all told her so. We especially praised her homemade blackberry cobbler. (Her way with lard crust was amazing. I tried to duplicate it in later years, but it was never as good as Mrs. Dutton's. I've often wondered if baking it in a coal-fired cookstove made a difference. Certainly the cold well water we drank seemed better than the "city water" the well-to-do people had.)

After supper and dishes, we set out for the downtown parade. We had to walk because we didn't have the 5 cents for streetcar fare, but we didn't mind. I can still hear the rattle of the streetcars and see the electric sparks flying from the friction on the overhead electric cables. We were "dirt poor" in material things, but rich in love and childhood happiness. I guess Darlene and I didn't even realize that we were poor.

Downtown, the streets were filled with people. The Halloween parade used to be almost as important to us as the Fourth of July parade. Those parades were good, clean entertainment for young and old.

The parade started, led by a red devil carrying his long, pointed tail over his arm. A smaller red devil behind him carried a pitchfork over his shoulder. Awed, we clung to our mothers.

We watched in amazement as an eerie white ghost fluttered by, keeping its distance from the devils. A witch wearing a black cape, a tall pointed hat and a toothless smile cackled diabol-ically as she followed the ghost, riding on her broomstick. Now and then she emitted a shriek that chilled us to the bone.

Darlene and I sucked in a breath as a huge spider crept along beside us, trying to avoid the tentacles of the octopus behind it.

A headless horseman on a black horse rode by, carrying his head under one arm—shades of Sleepy Hollow!

Not to be outdone, a snake charmer passed, a large snake coiled around her waist. The crowd shrank back as the reptile kept sticking out its flickering tongue. It was probably more scared of the crowd than we were of it.

After many more ghosts, goblins and gim-micks, an oversized pumpkin waddled along, passing out orange and black candy kisses to the children. What a sweet way to end a parade!

Darlene and I breathed a little easier after the parade ended. We started for home, cling-ing to our mothers as we hurried down the dark streets, visualizing ghouls behind every tree, waiting to grab us.

Once we reached home, our fears melted away like an April snow. I kissed Mother

goodbye at our door and kept close to Darlene and her mother, just in case. Mrs. Dutton quickly lit the kerosene lamp, and its flickering flame was most welcome. She also turned down Darlene's bed for us with a reminder that it was getting late, and we had to go to school the next day. We quickly put on our pajamas and jumped into the soft feather bed, drawing the warm quilt up to our chins.

"Good night, little angels, don't let any monsters in," Mrs. Dutton said with a chuckle.

"We won't," we promised, shivering as the wind started to howl.

We were just sinking into sleep when we heard a scratching at the window. "What was that?" I whispered to Darlene.

"Sounds like someone's trying to get in the window!" she whispered. As we lay frozen in fright, the noise came again, louder this time. We opened our mouths to scream, but nothing came out. I was finally able to whisper that we should slide to the floor and crawl to her mother's room. Darlene held my hand as we slid to the cold floor and started crawling.

The noise came again. This time, it was so loud that I thought the monster had surely broken the window. My scream brought Mrs. Dutton running with the kerosene lamp. We were so scared that all we could do was point to the window.

Mrs. Dutton ran to the window and lifted the shade while we tried to gasp out our story.

"There isn't anyone out there, darlings, but the wind has torn the window screen loose, and the wind is whipping it against the window," Mrs. Dutton explained. Ahhh—we could breathe easily now!

"Uh, Mother, would you like to lie down with us, please?" Darlene asked. "I think Selma is afraid."

"How about you, Darlene? Aren't you a little afraid too?" her mother replied.

Darlene looked a little sheepish. Our laughter broke the tension, and we relaxed as we moved over to give Mrs. Dutton room.

"Thanks for inviting me, darlings," Mrs. Dutton said, her sweet voice wrapped in a chuckle. Then two scared little girls sighed as the sandman wove his magic and transported them to a dreamland free of monsters. ❖

Halloween Fun

By Maralee Gerke

Halloween was always a simple but exciting fall ritual when I was growing up on a farm in Oregon's Willamette Valley. The 1940s were a simpler time; we had one car and no TV, so we were pretty isolated from other kids our age.

As Halloween approached, our excitement increased. We could hardly wait to carve the pumpkins in the garden—the ones in which Dad had carved our names as they grew.

Making costumes and masks was another favorite evening activity leading up to the holiday.

One of the best Halloweens was when my dad borrowed the open-back bean truck from the farm.

He filled it with hay bales, and we drove around and picked up kids from our far-flung neighborhood. I think some of the parents rode with us too. We then drove all around to the nearby houses and went trick-or-treating.

It was great fun to ride in the crisp fall air with our friends. We collected all kinds of great homemade treats that night—doughnuts and cider, freshly picked apples and popcorn balls. But the best thing about it was sharing an evening with friends from other farms.

Even though our treats were soon eaten, the memory of that Halloween has lingered. I can still see the smiles and hear the happiness in the voices of the children who rode in that truck on a cool October night 50 years ago. ❖

A Very Expressive Jack-o'-Lantern

By Kate Hartnell Stobbe

M y 4-year-old sister, Eleanor, and I sat on the front porch steps of our home in St. Louis County, eagerly awaiting Dad's arrival home from work. He had promised a surprise on this summery October afternoon. Our thoughts ranged from a sack of candy to a trip to a toy store. Naturally, we were on our best behavior.

At last, the family flivver eased up to the curb. Mother waved from the porch and said she'd be there in a minute. Soon we were loaded into the car and on our way. But we passed all the "surprise" destinations we'd thought of and headed out into the country.

We passed several farms, gaily waving and mooing at the cows and neighing at the horses. Finally Dad turned onto a dirt road and read a large, hand-painted sign: "Pumpkins For Sale."

Then Mother asked, "Do you know why we are here?"

I vividly remembered carving happy faces on pumpkins the year before.

"Yes!" we answered. It was almost Halloween, and we were there to buy a pumpkin or two from Dad's friend.

I was 6 years old that October in the late 1920s, and I vividly remembered carving happy faces on pumpkins the year before. I also remembered the delicious pies and muffins we had "helped" Mom make from the pumpkins' inner goodness. We exited the car to face a sea of plump, orange orbs to choose from. In fact, we were told, they represented 6 acres of plantings. Many already had been taken to the local general store to be sold on consignment.

Eleanor and I were told to each pick one that we'd like to turn into a jack-o'-lantern. My sister pointed to a monstrous pumpkin that surely weighed 50 pounds. We laughed at her ambitious, imaginative thinking. Then Dad pointed to the 3- to 10-pound section. Mother had no trouble finding two to fit her baking needs.

Some time later, Eleanor and I decided on the ones we wanted to carve. Then the owner of the patch showed us a stack of miniature pumpkins and said that we could each have one of those too.

We walked up to the farmer's porch to visit and pay for our Halloween decorations. The steps were lined with carved pumpkins, some smiling, some sad, others frowning. Some had blackened teeth. One wore a bow tie just below his toothy grin.

Hats adorned two of them. We wondered about candles; would the hats burn?

As Dad and Mr. Roberts talked, "Mrs. R," as everyone called his wife, gave us home-made cider made from apples grown in the nearby orchard.

Soon we were driving home, anticipating our jack-o'-lanterns' appearance. I had already decided to create a happy face on mine. Eleanor chatted away, never giving a clue as to her decision. But we would soon learn she had ideas of her own.

It was late when we arrived home. Dad suggested that we play a hand or two of Go Fish and do our carving in the morning, a Saturday. Playing cards and concentrating on the game, we completely put pumpkins out of our minds.

But the next morning, I awoke with carving plans spinning in my head. After breakfast, we descended the basement stairs to begin work on an oilcloth-covered table. My sister and I were seated on opposite sides. Mother wanted each of us to do our own creative thinking. Eleanor was given a small, rather dull knife. Being older, I was allowed a larger, sharper tool. My, how quiet it became as we went to work!

I drew a face on my pumpkin, changed it several times, and began carving. It turned out pretty much as I'd planned. Dad had already cut off the tops and removed the pulp. When I placed a candle inside, and it was lit, I was quite pleased with the result.

We patiently waited for Eleanor to finish her jack-o'-lantern. When at last she allowed us to look, I burst out laughing. Mom and Dad tried hard to keep from joining me as they patted Eleanor's head and told her what a handsome carving she had created.

The right eye of her pumpkin was at least ¾ inch higher than the left and much smaller. The nose took an upward turn and almost landed in the eye. The mouth swung off at an angle to the right of the nose with a single tooth close to the right gum line.

When a candle was lit inside, it revealed the funniest sight I'd ever seen. But Eleanor was completely oblivious to the humor. In her eyes, it was perfect.

Her jack-o'-lantern was proudly taken to Sunday school the following morning to enter in our church's annual contest. Did it win? You bet it did—for creativity.

Eleanor received a book of Bible stories as a prize. I was given a bookmark for my artwork.

But early Monday morning, Mother called the eye doctor to make an appointment for Eleanor. Eleanor was tested and was found to have perfect vision. There were no "up and down" problems with her eyes—only with her pumpkin's! ❖

Vintage postcard, House of White Birches nostalgia archives

Facing page: Halloween was twice the fun for Glen Herndon's girls back in the 1950s because the family always found room to grow their own jack-o'-lantern! They lit it with a big, fat candle inside. Looking down into it and watching the candle flame, they dreamed. In the photo are (left to right): Nancy, now a professional artist whose favorite illustrations are for Halloween; Michele, who became an ultrasound technician; and Janice, an osteopathic physician in Indianapolis, Ind. Photograph by Glen Herndon.

The Outhouse

By Timothy Daubert

I remember living with my grandfather, and I remember one night in particular. That's when my idea of trick-or-treating changed forever. The air was cold on our faces as we walked in the open field. The ground was soft from the previous night's rain, and the ground made a sucking sound as we walked, the black clay sticking to our shoes. It was Halloween night, and we were following our annual routine of pushing down outhouses. This year it was to be my grandfather's.

In our group of four boys was Donny, who had long black hair. Some of the girls found it attractive. He was the oldest. Robert played football at the local school. He was a large boy, very friendly. Chester was the first African-American in our school. His grandmother had been a slave.

And then there was me. I was 13. My mother had put me in an orphanage when I was 4. When I was 5, Grandpa had brought me to Alabama to live with him. The first time I saw him, I thought he was a giant because he was so tall and big.

We hit the outhouse with our full force, and it started to lean.

Outhouse, Spencer, Iowa, December 1936,
Photo by Lee Russell courtesy the Library of Congress

My grandfather showed me how to hunt and fish. We spent many nights camping along the Black Warrior River. As I lay on an old blanket, my grandfather would point out the planets and the stars.

He taught me that a man's word was his bond, and that I should never judge a man by the color of his skin. He taught me to live life to the fullest. He was a good man, and I loved him.

As we boys walked that Halloween night, we could smell the fragrance of orange blossoms. We could see the silhouettes of farmhouses, some of them more than 100 years old. The moon was full, and its light helped us see the slippery, sodden ground. As we came around the bend of the creek, the outline of the outhouse came into view.

As we approached it, we started to run, but the slippery clay would not allow us to get any traction. We shoved the outhouse, but it did not move. We backed up and tried again. This time, we hit the outhouse with our full force, and it started to lean. Finally it fell and slid into the creek.

All of a sudden, the door opened, and I could see the white hair on my grandfather's head. As the swift current of the creek carried the outhouse out of sight, I could hear my grandfather cursing loudly. Fear gripped me as I watched.

The other boys started laughing and rolling on the ground. "That was fantastic!" Donny said, tears in his eyes. After a few minutes of laughter, my friends went home. I left the scene with visions of my grandfather's white head floating down the stream.

I walked slowly back to the house and went to my room, where I waited in fear. I don't know how long I waited, but it seemed like an eternity.

Finally I heard the door open. My grandfather was home. My fear increased. But my grandfather did not come up the stairs. He turned out the lights and went to his room. I spent a restless night.

The next morning, I walked down the stairs as softly as I could. As I came to the bottom of the stairs, I could see my grandfather sitting at the table. He turned in my direction. The fear inside me increased as he looked at me with a stern expression.

He asked if I had been there the night before, and I said that I had been. Then he rose from his chair and walked toward me. I thought I was going to get a whipping, but he simply smiled and walked back to the table.

I don't know why he did not punish me. He did ground me for a month, and I had to help him put up another outhouse. He installed indoor plumbing later that year. A few months later, he died.

After the funeral, a friend of my grandfather's came to the house and told me why my grandfather had not punished me that day. He told me that he and my grandfather had done the very same thing when they were boys. ❖

It Was a Scream

By Joseph L. Theurer

When I was about 5 years old, we moved to a farm. I was the youngest of six children, and I had three older brothers and two older sisters. My sister Helen was the eldest. Next came my oldest brother, Bernard. Bernard was 13 years older than I was, and he always had a prank to pull.

On one warm, late-October day, Bernard seemed to spend an excessive amount of time in the outhouse. He said he was fixing a loose board. That evening, my parents had a masquerade party with lots of aunts, uncles, cousins and friends.

After the party started, we saw Bernard sneaking out. My brother Daniel, two years my senior, and I followed Bernard at a discreet distance.

It wasn't far to the outhouse. We watched as one of our aunts entered the little building. Then, 10 or 15 seconds later, she came out, screaming. We did not know what had happened.

Soon another aunt visited the outhouse. Daniel and I crept closer and spied Bernard behind a woodpile. He had removed one log so that he could observe the outhouse without being seen. We saw that he had run a pipe from the woodpile into the back of the outhouse, under the seat.

This time we were close enough to hear Bernard when, after 10 or 15 seconds, he spoke into the pipe: "Would you please move over? I am trying to paint down here while there is still some light."

And another aunt went screaming.

By this time, Mother got wind of what was going on. She knew that Bernard was behind it all, and soon she put a stop to his prank. ❖

The Halloween Prank That Backfired

By Faye Craig Hughes

For years we dreaded Halloween night. On that night, a group of boys—acquaintances of one of my brothers—would invade our neighborhood. They would wait until everyone had retired for the night, and then they would get busy.

First they would use their mother's home-made lye soap to blanket all of our windows. It took days to get it all scraped off.

Outhouse tipping was common, but the prank they loved most was putting a paper grocery bag containing fresh cow manure on a neighbor's porch near the door. They would knock on the door, then set fire to the paper bag and run away. The unsuspecting person would be so startled to find a burning bag near his door that he would stomp on it, splattering his feet and legs with manure.

One year Mom decided that we had had enough. We devised a plan to scare the boys so that they would never come back. My brother Grant, who had a vivid imagination and was a natural storyteller, went to work on the plan. He began passing the story around that our house was haunted. He recited an impressive list of the strange things the ghosts did. The wildest part was that one ghost could play the piano very well. According to Grant, we could hear the music and see the keys being depressed, but we couldn't see the ghostly pianist.

That part brought the biggest laugh of all. "Ha, ha!" they would chortle. "How funny! Who ever heard of a piano-playing ghost?"

Thus the stage was set.

The boys knew that we had an upright piano that was visible from the front windows. What they didn't know was that we had traded our old piano for a player piano. Players were not very common as yet.

On Halloween night, we turned out the lights as if we had retired early, leaving only a lamp burning near the piano. We had a piano roll in place hidden behind the closed doors at the top of the piano. A blanket covering the piano bench concealed my youngest sister.

"Look, fellas, there's that piano the ghost can play!"

We didn't have to wait long. When the boys arrived, one of them looked in and said, "Look, fellas, there's that piano the ghost can play!" They all burst out laughing. They pressed close to the window to get a better view—and at that moment, my sister began pumping the piano with her hands. In plain view of the boys, the music could be heard, and it did indeed seem that the keys were being pressed by invisible hands.

They dropped their bars of soap in fright as they made a fast exit. A few ran down the steps, but most just took flying leaps over the porch banisters. They were so convinced of the ghost story that they kept glancing behind them to see if they were being pursued by one.

The next day, we gathered up enough bars of soap to do our laundry for several weeks. One of the boys, we were told, burst into his parents' bedroom, white-faced and bug-eyed, babbling about seeing a ghost playing a piano. His dad got up and whipped him for lying.

And guess what? The boys never bothered any of us again. ❖

Ef You Don't Watch Out!

By Hazel Gray Miller

My brother, sister and I wore masks of thin, starched, clothlike material. Our costumes were old clothes. My brother, Ervin, dressed as a farmer's wife, wearing Mom's old housedress. My little sister, Gale, wore old overalls my brother had outgrown and a straw hat. She even carried a rake for her role as a farmer. My mask was that of a clown with red spots and a beard. I also wore patched overalls and a straw hat, and I carried a broom.

School children dressed in their homemade Halloween costumes. Mud Creek school, Cattaraugus County, N.Y., 1947.

At school, each class dressed up and paraded around the other classrooms. Most of the costumes were old clothes like ours, though a couple of kids had beautiful store-bought costumes. Some of my classmates made masks from brown-paper grocery bags, and old sheets were used for ghost costumes.

My parents did not allow us to go trick-or-treating, but we still had fun. We raised our own pumpkins, and on Halloween, we each carved a jack-o'-lantern. The pumpkin meat was scraped out so the outer shell was thin, and the deep golden flesh was made into three tiny pies. After the seeds were washed, Mom dripped bacon grease over them and popped them into the oven. Soon, golden pumpkin pies and crisp, browned, bacon-flavored seeds made mouth-watering Halloween treats.

The aroma of fudge wafted from Mom's kitchen as she made candy, and then popped corn and rolled sugared popcorn into balls. Mom didn't stop there; she made a place card for each of us and drew Halloween pictures on them. Each child had a place card as did she and Dad.

After supper, Mom set the big old galvanized washtub on the kitchen floor. We filled buckets with ice-cold water from the outdoor pump, then sloshed the water into the tub. Mom added some hot water from the teakettle so the water would not be too cold, and then we bobbed for apples. I got more water than I did apples as I tried to bite one.

We made a mess, splashing water onto the floor, but Mom didn't mind. She mopped up while we got into our nightclothes.

Dad worked the night shift at the mill. After he left for work, our spooky fun started. We blew out the flame in the kerosene lamp and lit candles in our jack-o'-lanterns. Then Mom gathered us around the crackling wood fire in our stove and told ghost stories, making them up as we talked. She capped off the evening by reciting James Whitcomb Riley's *Little Orphant Annie*. The exhortation that the goblins were going to get you "ef you don't watch out!" was enough to frighten me.

I must admit that I was scared by the time I went upstairs to bed. I even looked under my bed to make sure the two great big black things from the poem were not lurking there! ❖

Amos Sewell

The Trickster Tricker

By Haydn Fox

It was shortly before 1920. The custom of "trick-or-treat" at Halloween had not yet come into being. It was purely "trick" back then. In the area of Fern, Mich., about 8 miles south of Custer, farming was the main industry. Farm boys loved to play pranks on their neighbors. But one year, their antics were somewhat destructive to one neighbor's property. The angry farmer stormed that if anyone played tricks on him again, he was going to shoot them!

Such a threat was a challenge to my mother's three brothers, Glenn, Byrl and Cleal Huddlestun. When Halloween drew near, they schemed with a friend to dismantle a small horse-drawn wagon and reassemble it on the roof of a shed. This prank was often pulled in the Good Old Days.

Halloween came, and they were ready to make their move. All four had been gleefully looking forward to the evening. But alas, when the day arrived, Cleal, the youngest, became very ill. He lay there for most of the day, too sick to get out of bed.

As it grew dark and the time drew near for the boys to strike, the others went to Cleal's bed and let him know that they would miss him terribly. Cleal thanked them for their concern and encouraged them to proceed with the plans.

Then, shortly after his companions left, Cleal jumped out of bed, dressed and took a double-barrel shotgun from the gun closet. He then stealthily made his way toward the boys' destination, taking care to stay out of sight. Once there, he found a hiding place in some nearby bushes and waited.

Soon the two brothers and their friend had taken one wheel off the wagon and had started on the second. Cleal raised the gun and fired both barrels into the air. The boys panicked and ran away, terrified. Cleal quickly hurried home ahead of them. He put the gun in its place, donned his nightclothes and hopped back into bed.

As soon as the others arrived, they went upstairs to tell Cleal what had happened. Their clothes were torn and spotted with blood; in their haste, they had forgotten the barbed-wire fence that stretched a short distance from their victim's shed.

Cleal had to fight to keep from laughing. It was years before Cleal told them what he had done. Then they laughed too. ❖

Not for the Faint of Heart

By Elsie M. Creps

*A*s a child, I always looked forward with fascination to the mysteries of Halloween. I had visions of witches, ghosts and leering jack-o'-lanterns. The superstitions that surrounded the holiday frightened me, and yet they also fired my imagination. The sinister characters of the season seemed to loom everywhere.

We children really looked forward to Halloween. For one thing, most of the crops had been harvested by then, and Indian summer seemed to give everything a beautiful glow. Halloween was the very last time to celebrate before winter came upon us.

We ranked Halloween right after Christmas in importance, and we began planning way ahead of time to make it memorable. Our main goal was to scare someone.

Even years later, we still relished getting one of our family or friends to scream or holler in fear. And we let our imaginations run wild, thinking about how we could do it.

Back then, stores did not display so many outrageous costumes. We thought it was fun to make up our own creations. One favorite, a ghost, could be created by draping ourselves in old sheets with holes cut out for the eyes and nose.

We could also use sheets to costume ourselves as a mummy, Dracula, even a skeleton. Some years, though, we wound up dressing like a ragged hobo, an

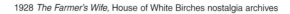

1928 *The Farmer's Wife,* House of White Birches nostalgia archives

Indian sprouting feathers, or a witch. For that last frightful character, we covered ourselves with dark cloth, made a witch's hat and rode around on a broomstick.

To hide our shapes and identities, we stuffed our clothes with leaves and painted our faces with black "makeup" scraped from the undersides of the stove lids on the old range.

After we married, the young people from church would come to our farm for their Halloween celebrations. One side of our corncrib was fixed up as a fun house.

Some of the community leaders would come out and work all day long, getting things ready. Every corner was decorated with cornstalks and jack-o'-lanterns. The candlelight glowing through the pumpkins' faces was the only light to be had in the fun house.

Apples were hung from the ceiling to knock the noggins of all who passed. Bats and ghosts fluttered overhead, and black cats hung over the windows. Those who decorated the barn tried to make the scene as eerie as possible.

As they entered the fun house, all the party-goers first had to walk a narrow plank and stumble over some loose, creaky boards. Then they got an electric shock with a pair of electric cow clippers that were run up and down their backs until they squealed and hollered.

Unnatural screeches and squeals were added by someone scratching on an old violin.

Then the visitors had their hands plunged into a bowl of "snakes"—cold cooked spaghetti. Next, their hands were put into a bowl of peeled grapes, which they were told were eyeballs. This brought more screams. Weird noises were heard at all times to make it as scary as possible.

Everyone had to shake hands with the biggest ghost after they left the place, and they were hit over the head with the witch's broom.

Afterward, there was plenty of food to enjoy—and that was good, for those who had endured the fun house had built up hearty appetites. There were lots of candied apples, apple cider, doughnuts, hot dogs and potato chips. We played games, such as bobbing for apples in a big tub of water.

A hayride always concluded the evening's festivities. It was the perfect final touch for a night they would always remember. The fun house was not for the faint of heart, but those who participated never forgot it. No fun house had more to offer than that one. The imagination of its organizers knew no bounds after they got their thoughts going.

Halloween has become an impersonal, pre-packaged, commercial event today. Children are taught to go and beg from door to door, and they call it trick-or-treating. But I think the pure fun of the season has vanished. I doubt that today's youngsters enjoy Halloween or look forward to it as much as we did back in the Good Old Days. ❖

A Halloween Ride

By Mildred McConnell

Mr. Farris had a wagon
Painted green, with wheels of red.
He just knew the boys would take it,
So Mr. Farris used his head.

Put the wagon in the barn lot,
Then put in some nice, soft hay.
Next he spread himself some blankets,
Then upon this bed he lay.

He woke to find the wagon moving,
Heard the boys whispering low,
Then at length they hit the gravel;
Now, he wondered where they'd go.

Three miles away, and in a creek bed
Swollen high with recent rain,
Mr. Farris stood up quietly:
"Now, boys, pull me home again."

And the moon shone
Bright as day,
So they pulled the wagon homeward
And 'twas uphill most the way.

Scared Stiff

By James D. Doggette Jr.

The Halloween scene of the early 1950s offered a cavalcade of special events on the south side of New Orleans. There were parties, public and private, as well as spooky yards and horror trails. But my friends, my younger brother and I chose good old trick-or-treating. It was no wonder, then, that Halloween was becoming our favorite holiday.

To us, "trick-or-treat" meant you got tricked if you didn't treat, and we had been notorious for our tricks—so much so that the grown-ups had dubbed us "the outlaws."

About a week before the grand night, Mama told us of a fantastic party that was to be held at our church, but that did not change our thinking in the least. We had long since decided that we would go around with our bags and collect copious amounts of goodies.

Visions of a bonanza of treats like candy apples, chocolates, cookies, popcorn balls, bubble gum and little bags filled with licorice, candy corn, suckers and gumdrops streamed through our minds day and night. We would have nothing to do with any alternate plan.

Spooky Halloween Mansion by J. Ducharme © 1970, House of White Birches nostalgia archives

At last Mama relented and agreed to let us go, with the usual parental guidance ringing in our ears. When the big night came, she brought us to our friend Ritchie's house. After visiting with his mom for a while, she left with my little sister and brother, telling us once again to be good and to listen to Ritchie's mom. We took off like a shot and began filling our bags.

Soon we came to a weird-looking house. No one knew that it belonged to one of my mom's best friends. We rang the doorbell and yelled, "Trick or treat!"

Suddenly the door opened to reveal an ugly old crone and her henchman, a horrific ghoul. She asked us what we wanted in a trill and rag-gedy voice, but we couldn't answer—the words seemed to stick in our throats.

Immediately she chimed, "Oooh, I know these nasty little boys! Look at this little plump one!" she said, pointing a bony finger at one of my friends. "We will put him into my pot and stew him with carrots and potatoes! Ah-ha-ha-ha-hah!" she cackled.

Lenny let out a wild, wailing scream and vanished. His bag full of goodies went flying into the air and came down with a whack, spill-ing the contents. We quickly followed him. All we could hear—besides the wind whistling in our retreating ears—was her screeching: "Get 'em, Igor! They're getting away!" That made us move even faster, if that were possible.

Like shooting stars, we separated, but we each made our way back to Ritchie's house. All the lights were out, and it was as silent as the grave, except for the knocking of our knees. Strange noises were coming from somewhere in the dark yard, and once again we were prepar-ing to set flight.

Just then, Ritchie's dad came out of the dark-ness. He was killing himself, he was laughing so hard. He carried a small black box that made a weird sound when he turned it.

Then Ritchie's mom turned on the lights, and we gathered around the front porch. My mom's best friend and her husband came around the corner to make sure we had gotten home OK. They had had a good laugh at our expense.

Before long, we were laughing too—espe-cially when we found out that Mom had helped plan the whole thing. ❖

The Stranger

By Margaret Winebarger

During the 1940s, my family lived in a government housing development in Newport News, Va. Daddy was with the Corps of Engineers, and he worked late hours, occasionally working out of town. Mother was left to take care of the five of us, ages 7–17, and manage the household in his absence.

She had a wonderful sense of humor and a spirit of adventure, and she frequently told us stories about her childhood and the daring feats she attempted. She had been a bit of a tomboy in her youth, and she loved to brag about her daring and the risks she took.

Back then, Halloween was a time for fun and excitement in the neighborhood. There were no concerns about walking down dark streets at night. Kids walked in little groups and did not have to be accompanied by adults. I was 7 years old, and along with my sister, age 10, and my brother, age 8, we were preparing for the spooky night ahead.

Our costumes were homemade. Mother usually found some old clothes for a "hobo" or a sheet for a "ghost." We weren't hard to please. We just looked forward to the treats and the scary night ahead.

One Halloween night, we noticed an unusually tall figure dressed in black, walk-ing slowly along the sidewalk ahead of us. It was frightening, and we were careful to keep our distance. But we were also curious to find out more about this mysterious figure. Finally, it disappeared.

When we got home, we told Mother all about it—and she started to laugh! The tall, dark figure we had seen was she! She held a broomstick over her head and had draped herself in black clothes. She loved adding a touch of mystery to our Halloween night!

I relive that night whenever I tell my own children about my adventure with the myste-rious stranger on that long-ago Halloween! ❖

An Unforgettable Date

By J. Norman McKenzie

A long time ago, when I was not quite 6 years old, I took part in a historic event. I was swept along in it and basked in a glow that yet lingers, although I was too young at the time to understand what it was all about or what great hopes surged up in mankind on that glittering night of splendor.

Even now, nearly a lifetime later, the picture is undimmed. I was playing in our yard in the small New England town of North Weymouth, Mass., that afternoon when my older brother and sisters came home from school. It must have been early because they had been "let out" to share the news.

I didn't know what the "news" was, but their festive air hinted that whatever it was, it must be very exciting. Years later, I learned that the news had spread like wildfire through the town, despite the fact that this was before the days of radio, and the telephone was a luxury only the wealthy could afford.

> *The news spread like wildfire through the town.*

In our neighborhood, as the news spread, people came out of their houses or left their jobs to huddle in groups, laughing and talking. Total strangers, so the story ran, stopped and shook hands. My mother, her eyes red, rushed outside to hug my father as he hurried home. (He, too, had been let out early, it seems.)

Dad brushed away Mother's tears, lifted her clear off the ground and swung her in a great circle. He grabbed her hand and mine, and we trooped into the kitchen, the other children romping alongside.

In my whole life I had never seen such joy.

When darkness fell, I was bundled into our old Model T (nobody had even thought about supper) and off we chugged to Thomas' Corner, the town square, where it seemed to my child's eyes that the entire world must have gathered.

To me, Thomas' Corner was the vital center of existence because that's where Mr. Jones had his store. It was what we would now call a convenience store, but to me it was the Taj Mahal of stores. I had been there often, mostly as a reward for not being naughty.

Facing page: These well-known recruiting posters—"I Want You" by James Montgomery Flagg—first appeared in 1917 during World War I. The original Army poster is inset on a lesser-known Navy poster. Posters courtesy the Library of Congress.

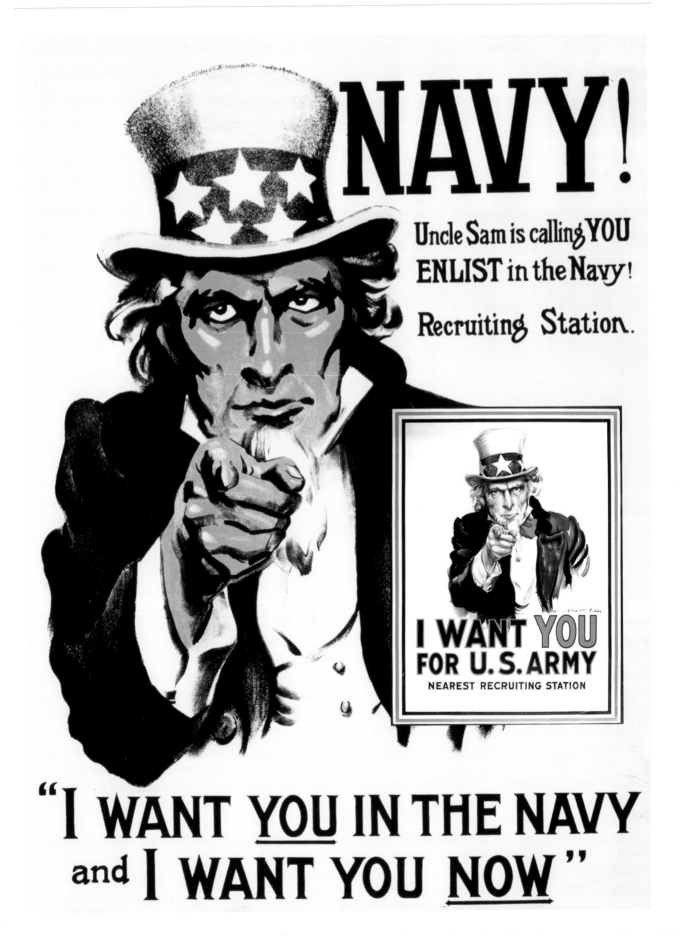

Sometimes my father let me tag along when he bought the Sunday paper. While he and Mr. Jones chatted, I ogled the wondrous stocks of penny candy in that sloping glass case. Mr. Jones was rich. He had to be—people handed money to him all day in exchange for all manner of things. (What puzzled me was why he would part with candy for mere money; it was another of the curious grown-up perversities that eluded my understanding.)

into Mr. Jones' store, leaving Mother and me outside, I was certain this night had a special wonder all its own. (Already, it was historic for me; I had never seen "the night" before, except from my bedroom window.)

The occasion became truly historic moments later, when Dad came out of the store with a box of chocolate-covered molasses chips, Mom's favorite. (I had no favorite, being partial to all kinds of candy.) The ultimate glory in this phantasmagoria of glories came when Mr. Jones himself suddenly appeared at the door of his store, clutching a double-barreled shotgun. He took aim at the sky. The gun exploded with a great roar, then another. Everybody cheered, and Dad gathered me in his arms and boosted me to his shoulders so I could see it all. How happy could one little boy be? And why weren't all nights like this splendid one?

Boy Scouts herald Armistice Day in a parade in 1920.
Photo courtesy House of White Birches nostalgia archives.

There I was, towering above the celebration, Mom at my side, my father's strong arms holding me aloft, my mouth crammed with candy, rich Mr. Jones laughing and joking the way I imagined all people of great wealth spent their days and nights.

Our route to the Corner (and Mr. Jones' store) on this night of splendor lay along the town's main street. As if by prearrangement, front yard after front yard blazed with kerosene cans, makeshift torches flickering in salute to whatever triumph had been achieved over the evil that had threatened. It was an eerie scene—as though we had stumbled into Dante's Inferno.

I was thrilled but frightened, and I snuggled up beside my father and reached out for my mother's hand just in case. (My older brothers and sisters were in the backseat, giggling and relishing the idea of being out after dark.)

Young as I was, I sensed that this was an occasion that was important and good.

When my father gave permission for the older kids to join some friends they had spied and then struggled his way through the throng

Little wonder that I sensed there would never again be a night like this, a time when all the world was wonderful, when everything anybody could hope for was within easy reach.

Years later, I came to realize that much of the grown-up world around me had held the same childlike view of the triumph that had brightened that spectacular night.

Time and its tribulations have long since tarnished that splendor. But on that monumental magical Monday night, which hailed the Armistice of Nov. 11, 1918, even the grown-ups reveled, just like that little kid with his chocolate-stained mouth. ❖

Armistice Day

By Frances N. Burnham

*I*t seems that the origin of Veterans Day has almost become lost in our vast country's history. I wonder how many young people today even know that it started with World War I, "the war to end all wars," and that the human cost of that war was nothing short of tragic. The four-year conflict involved 16 countries. It resulted in the deaths of 10 million soldiers and 8 million civilians, and 21 million soldiers were wounded. It ended with a cease-fire agreement, called an armistice, in the 11th hour of the 11th day of the 11th month in 1918.

To honor that victory, in 1919, President Woodrow Wilson named Nov. 11 Armistice Day. As Germany threatened the world again in 1938, Congress declared Armistice Day a federal holiday.

For the noble purpose of honoring all veterans of all wars, Congress in 1954 changed the name of the holiday from Armistice Day to Veterans Day. From 1971–1977, the holiday was observed on the fourth Monday in October, but then it was appropriately returned to its original Nov. 11 date.

Our family treated the holiday as a day to remember family veterans.

But long before Congress changed Armistice Day to Veterans Day, our family treated the federal holiday as a day to remember family veterans from every war. My great-uncle on my father's side, Edward Minor Pauley, served in World War I in Rapid Repair Unit 307 of the Motor Transport Corps; and my great-great-grandfather on my mother's side, William H. Brate, served in the 13th New York Regiment Heavy Artillery during the Civil War. We honored both on Armistice Day.

I was blessed to have two sets of grandparents, two great-grandmothers and one great-grandfather still living when I was growing up. In fact, I was privileged to actually live in the same farmhouse with four of them, and aunts and uncles. Consequently, I heard the old stories about my ancestors over and over, and it made me interested and patriotic at a very young age.

One particular Armistice Day stands out from all the rest. In the fall of 1940, I was 10 years old, and our country once again was worried about entering a world war with Germany.

One autumn day, P. Sheridan Smith, our school principal and seventh- and eighth-grade teacher at Thomas Corners School in the town of Glenville in upstate New York, came into our fifth- and sixth-grade classroom. He announced that there would be a piano contest, and that any pupil who could play *America* (or *My Country 'Tis of Thee*, as we often called it in those days) was encouraged to enter. The winner would have the honor of playing *America* in the Armistice Day assembly.

I lived with extended family on a secondary road in a large, 20-year-old farmhouse without electricity or indoor plumbing. At that time—the tail end of the Great Depression—we certainly did not have money for piano lessons. However, we did have an upright piano in the front hallway, and my mother had had a few piano lessons from a classmate when she was young.

As soon as I got home that day, I raised the top of the piano bench and searched through the music. I was happy to find *America* in one of the old music books. I tried hard to figure out

The author's great-uncle, Edward Minor Pauley, enlisted when World War I broke out and served overseas for two years, achieving the rank of lieutenant in the U.S. Army Flying Corps Reserves. After the war, he started Flyers Inc., the first commercial airline out of Albany, N.Y. He served that airline as its president and as a pilot. Born in 1895, he died at the age of 32 with two other pilots in Rural Grove, N.Y. He was a passenger on a Colonial Western Airways plane that crashed in heavy fog. He was buried with full military honors carried out by American Legion Post 472 of Johnstown, N.Y.

the notes, but I was not successful, so at my first opportunity, I asked my busy mother to teach me to play.

Her response was short and sweet. She pointed to middle C and told me to count from there, that I could figure it out by myself. I was a little disappointed by her response, but I wasted no time in following her advice.

The days were rapidly growing shorter and colder. Directly after school each day, I sat myself down at the piano, still wearing my coat, hat and mittens, to count the lines and spaces until the natural daylight faded from the only window in the long, wide hallway. I would study the notes until I had memorized them as best I could, and only then would I remove both mittens to struggle with the keyboard.

Figuring out the chords was difficult in the fading light of the gray November days. However, by working extra hard over the weekends, I finally mastered *America*—and just in the nick of time, too, as Nov. 11 was just around the corner. In the short time I had left, I would try to play it more smoothly—not so choppy.

I had not told my classmates that I was entering the contest. No one seemed to be talking about it anyway. My girlfriends actually took piano lessons from a teacher. They also had the luxury of practicing as long as they wanted in electrically lighted, well-insulated, centrally heated homes. I did not think I had a chance of winning. Then again, it truly was not winning that mattered to me; it was playing in the spirit of honoring all veterans.

On the day of the contest, we girls gathered in the school gym/auditorium in the basement, where there was a stage, folding chairs and an out-of-tune piano. The other girls were surprised to see me there; they knew that I did not take piano lessons.

Our two judges were Mr. Smith and the third- and fourth-grade teacher, Miss Elsie Koch, who could play the piano. They walked into the room together and called out the name of the first girl to play. I was the last to be called. I quickly sat down at the piano, trying not to let my nerves get the best of me. I took a deep breath, and my untrained hands took over from there. As if in a daze, I got through *America* without a mistake.

Afterward, I could not get back to my folding chair fast enough. I was greatly relieved that it was over.

We all waited to hear the verdict as the judges turned their backs to us to confer. When they finally turned to face us again, Mr. Smith announced that I had won the contest! No one in that room was more surprised than I was.

The next day, Mr. Smith called me out into the hall. He wanted me to hear it from him, and not from my classmates: The mothers of the girls who took piano lessons were furious that I had won.

But he then stated that taking piano lessons never had been a requirement of the contest. He also told me that he and Miss Koch would stand by their decision. I would play *America* in the Armistice Day assembly.

When assembly day arrived, I was really nervous about playing in front of the other children and our four teachers. Most of all, I was intimidated by the mothers' protests, even though no family members would be there.

But now I was obligated to play, so I forced myself to sit down at the keyboard. Somehow I managed to get through *America* without a single mistake—a small miracle, considering my state of mind.

I did receive an additional reward

back in 1940, on Armistice Day itself. I waited alone in our front room, next to our battery-operated radio, for 11 a.m. to arrive. When the appointed time arrived, during that moment of radio silence in respect for our country's veterans, I bowed my head, and the most wonderful sense of heartfelt patriotism swept over me.

Today, I can't help but wonder if the veterans were saying thanks to a 10-year-old girl who played *America* for them in the Armistice Day assembly. ❖

Photo, House of White Birches nostalgia archives

When Masqueraders Reigned

By Arthur Muller

Although we cannot all be actors, we do, at times, enjoy playing different roles. This longing for amusement and a change from the usual routine was gratified on many occasions during the early 1900s. One of the many holiday diversions was the so-called "ragamuffin" sidewalk parade on Thanksgiving Eve in the Yorkville section of Manhattan. Third Avenue was the scene for the colorful extravaganza, as men and women of all ages participated in a 6-mile march from early evening until midnight. Nothing else in New York ever surpassed the variety and beauty of the costumes, the fascinating pageantry and the merry-making this grand array of strolling celebrants displayed.

The parade started at 59th Street and proceeded north on the east side of the avenue. At about 89th Street, the procession crossed to the west side and marched south, back to the starting point. Of course, many joined the ranks at various points along the line of the march. The Third Avenue elevated structure dominated the center of the street, and it served as a dividing line between the northbound and southbound processions.

A group of city "farmers" usually led the parade.

A group of city "farmers" usually led the parade. Some carried live chickens, some pushed wheelbarrows or carried rakes, and some furnished country music with their fiddles for the city slickers as gingham-clad girls square-danced their way up the avenue.

Laughing clowns with their amusing antics were the highlights of the evening. These circus-act impersonators with their red noses and lavishly painted faces were a show by themselves. Some rolled barrel hoops while others performed somersaults and acrobatic stunts. They were constantly cheered by the spectators who lined the sidewalks on both sides of the avenue.

There were also pirates dressed in brilliant colors, brandishing their flashing swords. Bullfighting Spaniards waved their red capes. Turks and Arabs paraded in full regalia along with just plain cowboys and dudes. All of them contributed an international flavor on this festive holiday eve.

Feminine pulchritude was not to be outdone by the predominance of male characters. Gibson Girls of the Gay '90s, Cleopatra and Joan of Arc were joined by ordinary dainty damsels in homemade costumes. This latter group would join hands in a Paul Jones or minuet, soon to be guided by gallant males who whirled them around.

Barber parlors closed early on Thanksgiving Eve for the benefit of the barbershop quartets who sang their renditions of *O My Darling Clementine* and *She Was Only a Bird in a Gilded Cage*. Some of them even carried their private shaving mugs that displayed their names in gold lettering.

One or two Italian organ grinders with their monkeys joined the parade, cranking out *O Sole Mio* and *Come Back to Sorrento* in grandiose style. The three-piece German brass bands tuned up their tubas with *O Du Lieber Augustine* and the *Blue Danube Waltz*. Patriotism was at its height as soldiers, sailors and marines, marching in perfect formation, added dignity to the event with their banners and rifles.

Although this parade had been called "a ragamuffin spectacle," it was anything but that. While many persons made their own costumes, thousands rented elaborate cloaks, robes, gowns, suits and military raiment to depict various periods in history.

A few kings and queens of different nations passed by, an occasional royal pair preceded by their retinue of attendants. Had this parade marched in the street instead of on the sidewalks, wagons and coaches no doubt would have been included in the celebration. Even so, a few decorated bicycles and tricycles wove along slowly among the crowds.

Today we have many Thanksgiving parades, including Macy's in New York and the great Detroit, Philadelphia and Toronto parades with their spectacular floats. These are beautiful, but I miss the entertaining ragamuffin strollers who merrily strutted by in those Thanksgiving Eve parades on Third Avenue. They are the vanished masqueraders of a bygone era. ❖

Above: An old-time Macy's Parade advertisement from the days when children weren't the only masqueraders in New York City. Below: Giant balloons adorn New York City streets during Macy's Thanksgiving Day Parade in 1979. Photo by Jon Harder courtesy the photographer and Wikimedia Commons.

An Unforgettable Thanksgiving

By Raymond Bottom

Times in rural Kentucky in the mid-1930s were, as the residents described them, "awful bad." Money was too scarce in our family to spend on toys and entertainment, so a 10-year-old boy had to devise his own forms of amusement. One game I enjoyed was "road watching" people and vehicles on their way to town. Many of the vehicles were wagons whose "horsepower" was supplied by mules.

I would wave and yell greetings to passersby. Most would smile and wave without slackening their pace. But not Mr. Atchley. He would pull his wagon to the side of the road and talk to me. After we became acquainted, he would let me hold the mules' reins while I rode a short distance with him before he let me off.

I looked forward to Mr. Atchley's weekly trip to town. Often he had sacks of his farm-grown vegetables to give to Mother.

Mother told me for the umpteenth time to mind my manners.

In early November, Mr. Atchley told me that most of his family members were gathering at his home for Thanksgiving dinner. As he discussed all the enjoyable ways his family celebrated Thanksgiving, I blurted out, "I wish I could come!"

"We would love to have you, but what would your parents say?" Mr. Atchley said.

I spent the next week begging Mother's permission to go to the dinner. Her main concern was the trouble it would cause Mr. Atchley. He would have to make four trips of 5 miles each way with a team of plodding mules.

When I told Mr. Atchley about my mother's concern, he pulled the wagon into our yard for a talk. "Everyone in the family is looking forward to having Ray as a guest," he told Mother. He tousled my hair. "I reckon this boy is worth four trips and then some."

I watched anxiously for the sight of Mr. Atchley on Thanksgiving Day. While I was waiting, Mother told me for the umpteenth time to mind my manners. We rehearsed the phrases "Thank you," "Please pass the salt," "Yes, sir," "No, ma'am" and many others that would indicate I was a "well-brought-up boy."

Finally the wagon rumbled into our yard. I bolted out the door and clambered aboard, bundled against the chill November wind. As we rode to his home, Mr. Atchley told me who would be there, describing everyone as "fine folks." He told me his children were grown and would soon be getting married. Then he asked if, since he didn't have any grandchildren, it would be all right if I became his "adopted grandchild." I accepted the offer with joy.

When we arrived at the Atchley home, all the family were waiting to meet me. The women hugged me, and the men shook my hand in man-to-man fashion.

I had never seen so much food on one table—turkey, ham, mashed potatoes and gravy, sweet potatoes, biscuits, rolls, beans, corn, fruit dishes—and everything raised on the farm. A special dessert table awed me with the variety and number of cakes and pies it held.

After everyone ate too much of everything, there was talk, laughter, and family singing, accompanied by a few snores from some who were lulled to sleep by full stomachs and the warmth of a blazing fireplace.

Too early, it seemed it was time for me to go home. I went through all the goodbye hugs and handshakes, and told everyone how much I had enjoyed myself (just as my mother had instructed me).

When we arrived at my home, Mr. Atchley gave Mother some turkey, ham, rolls, a cake and pies. "We had too much," he told her, "and I don't want to be eating leftovers this time next week." Mr. Atchley grinned. "Before you ask, Ray remembered all his manners."

"I had a wonderful time, Mr. Atchley," I said as he turned to leave.

"Well, thank you, Ray," he said. "You were a wonderful guest."

Mr. Atchley proffered his hand, but I ignored it and gave him an affectionate hug. For just a moment, his strong arms enveloped me in a bear hug that I have never forgotten.

More than 60 years have passed since that memorable day. Now Mr. Atchley and his family rest in the same rural church cemetery where my mother is buried.

Each time I visit her grave, I stop by his tombstone, and I always say, "I had a wonderful time, Mr. Atchley." ❖

Over the River, Through the Wood

By F. Lemon Adams

The sun was just a bright spot against the lowering sky as we skimmed down the winding road—Dandy snorting and blowing, with sleigh bells jangling and hoofs sluffing in the dry snow, all in perfect symphony with the who-who-who-o-o! of the hooty owls across the river. I answered them, and we got a whole chorus of "Who-o-os."

"Don't see how you make all those animal sounds so they answer you," Fran said.

Fran was my older sister. She and my small brother, Little Mose, and I were joyfully on our way to Jeremy Young's place to bring him home with us for Thanksgiving dinner.

I hung over the side of the cutter as far as possible to watch the ground race past as Dandy, reaching out with long-extended front legs, seemed to be pulling the earth back under the cutter.

> *"I feel sorry for people who aren't riding through the woods like we are."*

"Hold 'er, Dandy! We'll get there soon enough!" Fran shouted over the rising wind. As we tore along, we waved hilariously to a man who was mending his gate. He waved back with even more enthusiasm until we were lost to sight by a curve in the road. Another man, his long red beard streaming out from his face like a banner, dropped his bucksaw and waved both arms at us until we were out of sight.

"I feel sorry for people who aren't out riding through the woods like we are," Fran said. As we raced along, sudden gusts swung in from the east, belting us with stinging snow, reddening our cheeks and numbing our noses.

"Guess nobody's gladder than we are!" Little Mose called into the wind, head tipped back, the better to see out from under his stocking cap.

He and I drew the fleecy robe up around our necks; how delicious to be so cozy warm in the presence of all this whipping cold!

All too soon we rounded the last curve, and there stood Mr. Young's tidy little house, set in a clearing, its back against a dense wall of cedar trees—a living windbreak that he had planted in years gone past.

"Well, here we are at Daddy Young's humble abode," Little Mose said solemnly. Fran and I laughed so hard that he crawled under the robe in embarrassment. Often the old gentleman had used the expression—but coming out of tiny Little Mose … !

Jeremy motioned from the door that he would be right out. At the same instant, a cloud of startlingly blue birds dropped from the sky, squalling, scolding, wheeling and dipping over the horse and cutter.

Little Mose disappeared under the robe again, but Jeremy hauled him out from under the seat and held him on his lap. He wrapped the broad skirts of his old-fashioned greatcoat around him and crooned, "Little ol' jays won't hurt nobody. They's the watchdogs of the woods. Was just a-telling of me you were out there. Just a-guarding of my home they was."

Home. Dandy knew we were headed back home. She took off, feet hardly touching the ground. Home, with its noisy bustle, where Ma would be hurrying from cookstove to sink; from kitchen table to pantry; from woodbox to kitchen cabinet—like the knight of old who leaped on his charger and rode in all directions at once!

There would be the enfolding cloud from the bubbling pots on the range, mingling the aromas of roasting goose, dressing, gingerbread and spicy pumpkin pies. But overriding the fragrant fog, the smell of baking bread. We were all thinking the same thing.

Fran slapped the reins sharply on Dandy's rump, and we tore up the drive with a flourish. She swung around in the back yard, cutting the curve too close, and over went the cutter, spilling us all into the snow. Little Mose, who had fallen sound asleep, looked up into Jeremy's face, asking, "Did those big birds sing their song just for me?"

"Sure an' they did," he nodded. We quickly righted the cutter. "You young 'uns get into the house. I'll put the horse up. Save me my place by the range … ."

A Boy's Thanksgiving Day

By Lydia Maria Child

Over the river, and through the wood,
To Grandmother's house we go;
The horse knows the way
to carry the sleigh
Through the white and drifted snow.

Over the river, and through the wood—
Oh, how the wind does blow!
It stings the toes and bites the nose
As over the ground we go.

Over the river, and through the wood,
To have a first-rate play.
Hear the bells ring, "Ting-a-ling-ding,"
Hurrah for Thanksgiving Day!

Over the river, and through the wood
Trot fast, my dapple-gray!
Spring over the ground
like a hunting hound,
For this is Thanksgiving Day.

Over the river, and through the wood—
And straight through the barnyard gate,
We seem to go extremely slow,
It is so hard to wait!

Over the river, and through the wood—
Now Grandmother's cap I spy!
Hurrah for the fun! Is the pudding done?
Hurrah for the pumpkin pie!

The wind plunged down over the roof, driving the rest of his words back down his throat. But we were already storming the back door. ❖

Anything for Thanksgiving?

By Betty L. Rosian

Trick-or-treating has always been a mystery to me. I don't know when or where it started. The closest thing to it when I was a child in New York City in the mid-1930s was called "begging."

In late November, children would dress up in whatever costumes they could manage—mostly ragamuffin outfits—and go from door to door, asking, "Anything for Thanksgiving?" An outstretched hand was usually rewarded with a small coin.

It was a fun time, even though my sisters and I were not allowed to beg. Mom would dress us in colorful costumes she had fashioned from crêpe paper, and we'd walk the neighborhood streets.

At the height of the Great Depression, money was scarce—in our home and others. It didn't seem fair that we could not take advantage of the generosity of those who could afford to give. Still, we enjoyed the game despite its limitations, and we looked forward to it each year.

One year, back when white clothes symbolized the medical profession, I was dressed as a doctor, and my sister Alma was dressed as a nurse. Mom pinned white bands with small red crosses to our sleeves. Then she pinned another around our dog, Mitzi, and attached a little tin cup to each side of her, in the style of the standard Red Cross appeal.

Taking Mitzi's leash, we set off down the street, feeling very snappy indeed. Mom's firm warning "No begging!" rang loudly in our ears.

Then it happened—purely by accident, you understand. A woman passing us on the street dropped a nickel into one of the cups and walked on.

Alma and I froze, looking at each other in horror. What would we do with the money? It would never do to go home with it. How could we possibly explain it? But it was too much money to waste. The only reasonable solution was to get rid of it. We huddled in debate.

A nickel was not easy to spend. We were used to getting the same things, and 5 cents was not divisible by two. A malted milk cost 3 cents; couldn't get two of those. A dill pickle out of the big, pungent wooden barrel cost 2 cents. That would leave a penny. Another dilemma! Candy was bad for our teeth, we had been told, so that was not a consideration.

Then Alma had a brilliant idea. Why not get one malted and one pickle and share them? It would work mathematically, but it might be dangerous. Mom had clearly warned us that malteds and pickles eaten together would give us appendicitis. Would they? Inquiring minds wanted to know.

Besides, at that moment, appendicitis seemed preferable to the bawling-out we'd get if we took the nickel home.

An hour later we returned home with empty hands and clear consciences. And a little more wisdom. The penalty for breaking house rules was too steep.

Even though we were never caught, we both agreed it wasn't worth the risk. ❖

Thanksgiving 1935

By Doris Saigeon

The first Thanksgiving I remember was 1935 in Ferron, Utah. We were all in Mama's kitchen and Mama was stirring the gravy. Gramma Bohleen was mashing white, fluffy mounds of potatoes. I sat on the wooden box by the kitchen window, smelling the chickens cooking (nobody in Ferron ever ate turkey for Thanksgiving in those days), the mincemeat pies in the warming oven, and the sage in the homemade dressing.

Later I helped carry the candied yams, jeweled molds of cranberry sauce and plates full of steaming-hot rolls to the dining room table where the menfolk talked and smoked and generally waited, smiling a lot, for the meal to begin.

I can't remember anyone saying a blessing, perhaps because the women were still busy waiting on the tables, and the men were not the church-going sort. But we were plenty thankful and really happy.

I helped carry the candied yams and cranberry sauce to the table.

After dinner I escaped out into the front yard where Uncle Bob was tossing a football to us. He was a real hero to me, being only three years older, but a lot wiser and more worldly. I was glad when he threw the ball to me; he laughed when I dropped it, so it didn't bother me. I picked the ball up and threw it back.

Helen and Patsy were outside, too, but they were not really old enough to play football. The neighbor boys came over, and we three girls sat on the porch, bundled against the brisk winter wind in sweaters, scarves, woolen gloves and long stockings.

In the kitchen, the women did the dishes as they gossiped and laughed. In the living room, the men talked and smoked Bull Durham in hand-rolled cigarettes.

I wished I were a boy and old enough to play football. Patsy picked up one of Mitzy's kittens and held its fluffy body close to her chest. Helen did not sit still for long. She ran around whooping and hollering and cheering the boys on. Before long, she was too warm for the scarf and the sweater. Tossing them aside, she got right into the fray and tumbled with the neighbor boys, who tolerated her in good spirits, even though she did get in the way. They tried not to push her too hard, and once in a while, they handed her the ball and sheltered her while she ran a touchdown.

As the afternoon wore on, I got cold and went back inside and listened to the women talking about all sorts of things. For the most part, they didn't notice I was there unless the subject was too intimate for my ears; then they held their fingers up to their lips and said, "Sh-h-h, little pictures have big ears."

I was offended, and I moved into the living room, where Daddy picked me up and tossed me into the air a few times until I squealed "Uncle!" Then he set me on his bony knee and let me dangle there until I got a backache. Then I went on back outside for the last part of the ballgame.

Patsy got sleepy and was put down for a nap. Mama finished the dishes, and Gramma put them away. Aunt Christy and Uncle Bob gathered their three children and went on home to Emery, about 6 miles from Ferron.

They drove off in their big shiny car; Bob was quite well off and had a large farm and a lot of cattle and could afford new cars about every three years.

Gramma and Grampa Bohleen walked on home, down the hill a couple of blocks. Mama let me sit in her comfortable lap, and she rocked me back and forth in the black wooden rocking chair in the kitchen while Helen watched, waiting her turn.

Daddy put on his big sheepskin coat and huge Stetson hat and went out to milk the cows and feed the livestock. It was unusual to have Daddy home; he herded sheep down under the ledge in Colorado most of the year, and only got home for the holidays.

As I snuggled against Mama's warmth, I was sure that this was the best Thanksgiving Day I had ever had or would ever have.

I didn't know then that it was just one of dozens that would play out over the years—

with the same loved ones, the same menu and the same football games, which eventually I was able to join.

The war came and went. Uncle Bob went away to the Army and fought and came back safely. Gramma Bohleen lived to be nearly 100 years old. Grampa went home to heaven a little sooner, but he also lived a long time, as did Mama and Daddy.

My goodness, what memories that Thanksgiving of 1935 has stirred up! Now I am Grandma, and my kids and grandkids visit me.

The Thanksgiving chicken has been replaced by turkey, but everything else remains much the same. ❖

1954 *Wee Wisdom*, courtesy Janice Tate

John Slobodnik

Celebrations of Winter

Chapter Four

Back when I was growing up, I yearned to "stay up like the big kids do." That meant I wanted to push my bedtime to just as late as I possibly could. I have no idea who those "big kids" were I always referred to when arguing my case to Mama and Daddy; my big brother, Dennis, five years my elder, had the same bedtime as I.

Today I'm sure that bedtime would seem tame. From my earliest memories it seems it was around 8 p.m. in the winter; in the summer it was as soon after sundown as Mama could get us in from play or chores, cleaned up and bedded down.

In my early teenage years I succeeded in pushing it to 9 p.m. with the argument I needed the extra hour during high school days for completing homework assignments.

But Daddy was a firm believer in the Franklinism: "Early to bed, early to rise, makes a man healthy, wealthy and wise." Daddy was always in bed no later than 9 p.m.; he saw no reason why his progeny should be up later. Still, I yearned to "stay up like the big kids do."

I got my chance one New Year's Eve. My folks were going out to a party somewhere, a rare occasion for them in those days. Grandma was staying with us three kids.

I don't know what possessed Daddy to say it, but when Grandma asked what time we should be in bed, he replied, "I guess they can stay up until we get home."

I knew I had arrived!

I'm sure I protested, "But I want to stay up like the big kids do.

Mama and Daddy wouldn't be home until they had Auld Lang Syned in the New Year and that would be midnight. Finally I would get to "stay up like the big kids do."

Of course, there was little television to watch, and it seemed there was nothing very exciting on the Philco radio—what with the holiday and everything. Donna was the first to succumb, a little after 9 p.m. Dennis was next, about an hour later. I was left alone in my bleary-eyed effort to "stay up like the big kids do."

I don't remember much else. Grandma either was touched by my valiant battle against sleep, or was just too weary to put me in bed herself. At any rate, the next thing I knew there were muffled, dreamy voices and I was hoisted in Daddy's powerful arms and carried off to the bedroom. As he tucked me in, I'm sure I protested, "But I want to stay up like the big kids do."

Many years have gone by since. Daddy's way stuck with me, and I'm the most content today when I'm "early to bed, early to rise," with the exception being when Janice and I raise a New Year's toast and maybe even put on silly party hats.

We raised our own three children with a 9 p.m. bedtime—a bit old-fashioned, I'm sure, for the television generation. I heard many youthful complaints the equivalent of "I want to stay up like the big kids do," but they were to no avail.

I just smiled inwardly, remembering my own futile attempt on that New Year's Eve back in the Good Old Days.

—Ken Tate

John Slobodnik

A Homemade Christmas

By Robert Griesinger

Christmas was coming! Christmas was coming! Our snow-covered home was warmed by the holiday delights that were baking for that Christmas in 1930. I was 7, and the warmth of our family Christmas filled my heart. The treats gave off a nose-twitching fragrance. Dorothy and I watched, mouths drooling, awaiting a sample of Mom's specialty—sugar cookies.

Mom removed the hot goodies from the oven and laid them, one by one, on cheesecloth towels she had spread out on the table. Later, Mom decorated them with homemade frostings. Dorothy and I wiggled on our chairs as we sat and watched, hoping for a taste while the cookies cooled. The frosting on the cookies tickled our tummies deliciously.

Christmas was coming! Christmas was coming! As Dorothy and I looked at the Christmas tree, we smelled the scent of pine needles.

> *Our father was the supreme artist when it came to popping corn.*

This majestic greenery adorned a special place in our living room. What a pleasant reminder of what was to come!

Mom came into the front room with a pan of bright red cranberries, a large needle and heavy red thread. We watched as she pierced the cranberries, one by one, and strung them on the thread. When she had finished, we helped her hang the berry garland on the tree. These royal red strings would soon be accompanied by strung popcorn.

Our father was the supreme artist when it came to popping corn. The oil had to be just right, with a slight smoke rising from the pan, as he held the handle away from the gas burner. The sound of kernels popping inside the covered kettle—*rat-a-tat! rat-a-tat!*—filled the air. Then, wearing gloves, Dad took the steaming-hot kettle off the burner to let it cool awhile. Once cool, the white, fluffy morsels were strung, then draped on the tree. What a lovely contrast—dark green branches adorned with rows of white popcorn and red cranberries.

I can still hear our parents: "It's time to write your letters to Santa Claus before bedtime. Dad and I will help you send them tonight."

Dear Santa,

It was so nice to visit you at the department store. I liked your beard. I felt good sitting in your lap and talking to you. I gave you my list, so you know what I want this year to come to our house.

Facing page: *A Homemade Christmas* by John Slobodnik, © House of White Birches nostalgia archives

I hope I didn't ask for too much. Thank you. I hope you like the cookies.

Love, Bob

We dressed warmly before going out into the snow-covered front yard. Snow had been falling, giving the appearance of a white mantle. The soft glow from the porch lights helped my sister and me complete the next task—throwing breadcrumbs onto the ground.

"Now, place your letters on the snow so Santa's birds can fly them to the North Pole. This way, Santa will get them before Christmas," Mom sang out. Dorothy and I laughed as we imagined the birds picking up our letters in their beaks and flying them to the North Pole.

We looked at our parents, knowing it was late. My sister and I waited anxiously for them to nod their approval for what we wanted to do before going back inside. "Go ahead," they said, "but make it quick."

Dorothy and I fell onto our backs into the new snow. Flinging our arms and legs back and forth, we made an imprint in the white icing—angels in the snow. Our arms shaped their wings while our legs formed their gowns. When our angels were finished, Mom and Dad used the broom to brush the snow off us.

We had a warm bath and a cup of steaming hot cocoa before we were helped into our beds. We usually took turns having our four-footed friend sleep with us, and even though it was Christmas Eve, we had the same argument: "It's my turn!" The matter was resolved silently as our friend's tail wagged wildly.

Christmas was coming! Christmas was coming! The night seemed to last an eternity. We thought we heard sleigh bells and tiny hooves on the roof. But these sounds soon faded into darkness. Oh, we wished that morning would come!

Christmas Day! Christmas had come! The memories are still warm, the family still together. Gifts? Yes! But it was the support of one another that was the true gift.

Dad, dear Dad, was the only one who tried the patience of our family each and every Christmas. We smiled as he opened each gift in slow motion. Dad used his pocketknife to loosen the wrapping, being careful not to tear the paper. Very carefully, he folded the wrapping and laid it aside. Then, and only then, did he open the gifts, just as carefully.

But we were very cruel, ripping the wrapping quickly and tossing it aside. Oh, yes! "Thank you, Mom and Dad, for having Santa bring us these gifts!" That custom was fulfilled as my sister and I enjoyed our wonderful gifts.

Dorothy and I looked forward to dinner on Christmas Day. We knew it was a dress-up occasion, a special event in our dining room.

Mom had us help set the oak dinner table. We placed the white linen tablecloth, then the good china, while Mom watched the whole time. The silverware was in an antique box. Each piece was placed just so. We put the floral china plates next to the silverware in proper settings in front of each chair. The linen napkins had been folded from the last formal dinner; we set them in place last of all.

We watched as our parents brought in the food. The ivory gravy boat was filled with thick, brown gravy. The large tureen held mashed potatoes, and there were steaming bowls of vegetables, remnants of our summer garden. The crowning glory was the brown-crusted chicken, courtesy of the chicken coop in the far corner of our back yard. And for dessert, we had homemade mincemeat pie.

Mom's face was red from the warmth of cooking over the hot stove. She always wore her lace apron on special events. Dad sharpened the bone-handled carving knife, preparing to offer up the sacrificial chicken. Then from the oven came the chestnut stuffing with bits of onions and celery, moist and m-m-m good.

The soft glow from the crystal chandelier overhead warmed our hearts with laughter and joy. It was a special time, a special day. We appreciated a warm meal amidst the hardships of the times.

Christmas 1930 was wonderful despite the uneasiness of the outside world. My parents wanted to make it special, and it was.

It was a homemade Christmas. ❖

Chocolate-Covered Cherries

By F. Ramsey

Back in the 1920s, I was a small child living in Portland, Ore. Ours was a large two-story home. It included a room that we called "the library" (it would probably be called "the family room" today). Our Christmas tree was always in the library, and it was always a huge tree, right up to the ceiling and covered with all kinds of decorations, even though the candles were never lit.

My sister and I were never allowed in the library until the tree was all trimmed. We were told that Santa Claus was decorating the tree, and we must not peek. One time, we actually heard bells jingling outside while we waited in the dining room. We were certain it was Santa's sleigh.

After Santa completed decorating and had left his packages, the library door was opened, and we saw the beautiful tree. Each year it was prettier than the year before. One year, we got our first electric tree lights. They were beautiful, with little tinsel reflectors behind them and a gadget that made them flash on and off.

We always opened our presents on Christmas Eve, and we took turns, opening our gifts one by one so that we all could see what each person received. Mother always got slippers and a box of chocolate-covered cherries. She loved them, so that's what Daddy got her each year.

One year, he must have had a great deal of fun buying the candy, as there were at least *10 boxes* of chocolate-covered cherries—all sizes, shapes and brands. He had been to every store in town, and he bought each different box he could find. ❖

The Little Red Rocking Chair

By Bernice Vlahakos

After a couple of years of barely scraping by on the dairy farm, we moved back to Minneapolis. My dad tried to get back in at the post office, but the situation wasn't too good. He got a series of part-time jobs. That was a hard year.

My sister Loraine had graduated from high school and had joined us. She found it hard to get work in those Depression times. She finally got a job working for nothing but car fare, just to get the experience.

My mother had warned us that Christmas would be just another day that year—no gifts, no tree, no fancy meal and no sending Christmas cards. However, Loraine decided to do something special. She walked to work one day a week, saving a little money until she had enough to buy a gift for my little sister.

When Loraine brought home a little red rocking chair as a Christmas gift for Bev, it inspired all of us. Erle and I tried to think of what we could do for gifts for everyone that wouldn't cost anything.

My brother and I wrote notes to the others, telling them what we would do for them as a gift: "I will shovel the snow for you without being asked." "I will babysit Bev for you whenever you want me to." "I will do the dishes for

Beverly Lundeen.

you when it's your turn." And so it went.

When Christmas Eve came, Loraine brought out the little red rocking chair for Bev. "It's for you, honey. It's your Christmas gift."

Bev was too little to say much. She just stood there with big, round eyes. Finally, she touched the chair. It rocked a little. "Ooh," she said, her mouth making an "O." She rocked the chair again. Then she smiled until her dimple showed. Then she walked around the chair and looked at it from all sides.

"Why don't you sit on it?" Loraine coaxed.

"Me?"

"Yes. It's for you. It's your Christmas gift."

Finally she sat down, rocked a little, rocked some more, then rocked again. She beamed at us all. We all beamed too.

Then Erle and I gave our notes to everybody. We were all feeling better. Mom talked about the real meaning of Christmas. We sang *Happy Birthday, Dear Jesus.* Dad got his Bible and read the second chapter of Luke to us. We had crackers and soup, and we sang all the Christmas carols we could remember.

Mom said, "Why don't we get up early and go to the *Julotta* service at the nearby church?"

It turned out to be the Christmas I remember best: the Christmas of the little red rocking chair. ❖

Exactly as It Was Meant to Be

By Mary Sherman Hilbert

Christmas was always white on the prairie—white magic for children, white treachery for animals and travelers. Snowbanks 10 feet high had seemingly been designed by a whimsical, hibernal architect who contoured the land; here a cozy cave, there a miniature crystal castle where we knew winter fairies dwelled. Powder-sugar mountains rose to be climbed and conquered.

Right off the barn, we could slide, my brother and I, on homemade sleds of solid wood that sailed like the wind. We played thus until the cold numbed our fingers and toes, propelling us into the blissful warmth of the kitchen—to Mother and Ovaltine and steaming fresh bread.

Christmas was singing old familiar carols—in a country church if the roads were passable, at home if they weren't. It was the unbearable excitement of the annual program in a one-room schoolhouse heated by a balky coal furnace that drove a steady succession of teachers out of their minds.

Months of rehearsal and hubbub preceded those hours when we ached with suspense long before the burlap curtain rose. Each child had a part to play, regardless of talent—even the reluctant few who had to be dragged onto the stage. Our parents expected it. The real hams had leading roles or performed solos, and suffered ego displacement for months.

Christmas was patient fathers hitching faithful horses to buckboard sleighs piled with straw and fur robes. Patient mothers bundled children against the frigid cold, heating bricks for the 2-mile ride, praying for a windless night. Missing the program was unthinkable.

The blizzards that streaked across the treeless prairies turned the world into a frightening blur—"graybeard days," we called them, because "we couldn't see through Grandpa Winter's whiskers."

But there were also "Jack Frost days," when the earth was touched with a magic wand; "goose feather days" that quieted man and beast with a gentle hush; and magnificent, "azure-and-white days," when the sky was as blue as God's eyes, and the pure white earth shimmered like diamonds carelessly cast for the whole world to share—the world of a child's horizons—and the sweet arctic air filled your lungs till they were like to burst.

Christmas was a new doll every year from a live-in grandfather who never knew he was special folk. It was the blessing of family, ours and our best-friend neighbors who had eight children. The hustle and bustle was warm and wonderful because we loved one another.

Christmas was the discovery that Daddy was Santa Claus; thereafter Santa, Dad and Grandfather blended into one special folk who bestowed treasures on The Day: dolls, skates, sleds, a bicycle, a black-and-white puppy, a new baby brother!

Christ's day in 1903 was exactly as it was meant to be. A song in the heart, a star in the memory that flickers and fades but never dies. A very special day. ❖

Now Is the Time For Christmas

By Dale Simmons

Last weekend, I read an article in which a noted psychologist said that daydreaming is beneficial. That came as no great surprise to me. For years I've derived pleasure and relaxation from mentally reliving episodes of my childhood. Daydreaming provides an escape from the pressures of daily life, and for me, it has a tonic's effect. Herein lies a tale.

It was typical October weather in Saskatchewan. September's lavish colors had faded to somber shades of brown, and the sky was quilted with pewter clouds. It was a transitional time of year, neither fall nor winter. Even the precipitation was mixed; one minute there'd be rain, and the next, a snow flurry would intrude, huge flakes wafting down to disappear on contact with sodden lawns and puddle-riddled streets.

The day needed something to brighten it up. After a little thought, I hit on just the right solution. I'd sort through my horde of Christmas ornaments and make an early decision on which ones to use.

> *As I lifted away layers of packing, I rediscovered decorations that had belonged to my grandparents.*

The decorations filled a half-dozen large boxes, and as I moved them from storage into the living room, a delicious tingle coursed through me: Christmas was coming! It had been years since I'd taken complete stock of the ornaments, and the task became almost like a treasure hunt. As I lifted away layers of packing, I rediscovered decorations that had belonged to my grandparents, and ornaments my mom and dad had bought when I was a child.

I found exotic glass birds that predated World War I and the electric bubble lights that were all the rage in the 1950s. Artificial candles shared a chocolate box with the sparkle-covered silhouettes of reindeer; and in a battered biscuit tin were the china figurines for the Nativity. There were dozens of other ornaments as well, ranging from plain glass balls and paper bells to platoons of wooden soldiers and schools of cardboard carp.

In the last box I found three objects swathed in tissue paper. I had found a trio of childhood friends: a teddy bear, a patchwork clown and a plush Scotty dog with mismatched button eyes. Their discovery opened a Pandora's box of dormant memories, and I permitted myself the luxury of letting those memories transport me back to my childhood.

Facing page: *Bringing Home the Tree* by John Slobodnik, © House of White Birches nostalgia archives

Each year around mid-November, our Christmas-card list was brought out, and the pleasant task of preparing for the holidays began. It wasn't unusual for us to post more than 100 Christmas greetings. But then, in those days, quality cards could be purchased for a nickel each and mailed for 2 cents.

With the cards done, we'd launch our next major project: selecting our Christmas greenery. Artificial foliage and Scotch pines never caught on with us. Every year, there was real holly and mistletoe to dress the interior of the house, and we always had a cedar wreath to hang on the front door. Family tradition also dictated our choice of tree—it was a Douglas fir—and selecting just the right one was an adventure.

Private entrepreneurs cut the trees in the far north and trucked them into town early in December. Dad and I were among the first to meet them, and it wasn't uncommon for us to spend half a day sorting through the trees.

The object was to find the fullest, most symmetrical 6-footer in the bunch. Once our selection had been made, the tree was taken home and stored in the woodshed. Subzero temperatures kept it fresh until it was brought indoors and decorated.

As December progressed, excitement lent speed to the tempo of preparations. Mom busily finished her Christmas baking. By the time she was done, our pantry shelves fairly groaned under a delicious burden of sugar cookies, hand-dipped chocolates and fruitcake.

We all scrambled to take care of last-minute shopping and then double-checked to make sure everything was ready for the big day. For us, Christmas Eve embraced all of Dec. 24. From early morning till late at night, the house was a hive of activity. Friends and neighbors dropped by to deliver gifts and partake of Christmas cheer. The tree was brought in from the woodshed to thaw out. Dad would stand it in a bucket

filled with rocks and gravel, and while we waited for the branches to drop, we'd unpack ornaments and check lights for defective bulbs.

Bedtimes were relaxed on Christmas Eve. We'd have an early supper, then spend the later hours trimming the tree and listening to carols on the radio. Once the last bit of tinsel had been draped and the last icicle hung, we'd arrange our gifts around the base of the fir, then settle back to enjoy its splendor. After even the most critical evaluations, the consensus was always the same: *This* tree was the most beautiful ever.

Next came the ritual hanging of the stockings. Since our house didn't have a fireplace mantel, we used the mahogany sill that stretched 6 feet across the base of our living room window. Then, once the table had been set with Santa's refreshments, we trundled off to bed and the pretense of sleep.

Our household got an early start every morning, but especially on Christmas. Long before dawn, my parents would be up, tending to obligatory winter chores. Mom saw to the kitchen stove and prepared breakfast while Dad fired up the furnace. He'd clear the ashes, unbank a bed of embers and shovel in the coal. The sounds rumbled through the heating ducts that honeycombed the house and roused the rest of us.

Fitful slumber was quickly banished by the racket and by the realization that this was Christmas morning. The predawn chill went unnoticed as we scrambled into dressing gowns and stampeded downstairs. We weren't allowed to open any of the gifts under the tree until after breakfast, but we were permitted to empty our stockings. The nuts, oranges, ribbon candy and small toys only whetted our appetites for what was to come. Mom understood this and did not prolong the torture by trying to force a large breakfast on us. A slice of toast and a glass of milk were deemed sufficient.

As soon as everyone had eaten, we adjourned to where the tree and its treasures awaited us. We took our time opening gifts so each could be admired and appreciated. Long before we'd explored all the packages, daylight would be streaming through the windows. This was the

signal for us to bundle up and see to chores. Christmas Day or not, work had to be done.

With the eggs gathered, the cows milked and all the other livestock tended to, we'd settle down to a proper breakfast and a day full of Christmas fun. We became familiar with new toys and tried on the clothing we'd received. We helped with preparations for dinner and then ate ourselves into a pleasant stupor. Then we pitched in when help was needed to do dishes and clean up.

The day rapidly developed into a busy, happy and very special time. The only problem was, it sped by much too fast. As evening approached, weariness eventually overcame excitement, and albeit reluctantly, we kids permitted ourselves to be tucked in. We drifted off, however, knowing that while the climax of Christmas might have passed, action-packed days still lay ahead. There were visits to be made and more visitors to be welcomed; there were mounds of holiday treats to be leisurely devoured; and we hadn't yet begun to enjoy our gifts.

> *The day rapidly developed into a busy, happy and special time.*

For us, Christmas didn't end at midnight on Dec. 25. The holiday tapered off gradually and gracefully, and left everyone comfortable in the knowledge that it would soon return.

A glance through the living room window brought me back to reality. It also revealed that the weather hadn't brightened one bit. My mood certainly had, though, and I was of a mind to have Christmas start immediately.

I began work on my card list, and I dug out the catalogs so I could search them for gift ideas. This year there'd be no last-minute dashing about with panic buying. This year I'd make time to enjoy the slow buildup of excitement.

As I looked at the ornaments, I made another decision: This Christmas, every one of them would be put on display. I'd hang as many as possible on the tree and fill vases with the rest. I'd assemble the crèche. And my three old friends, the bear, the clown and the Scotty dog, would get places of honor on the mantel. It was the least I could do; they'd come a long way down memory lane to spend another Christmas with me. ❖

Christmas Also Meant Fireworks

By John Ray Cofield

Christmas was many things to us in rural Randolph County, Ala., when I was growing up. There were parties, hunts, visits, dances, gifts and fireworks to name a few. We did well to get a full week for our school holidays, as our parents wanted us out early in the spring to help with all phases of farming. This time, then, was certainly celebrated and enjoyed by all us young people to the fullest.

The Christmas spirit struck us many days before we actually were dismissed for the holidays. Our teachers always made great effort to decorate the classrooms in a festive and colorful array with decorated trees in every room. Boughs of cedar and pine mixed with holly and mistletoe added a festive air to many of the rooms. Red and green paper chains were draped and strung just about everywhere.

Some teachers pasted holiday designs—usually red candles or poinsettias—directly onto the window glass (I haven't seen this done in years and years, however). Other cutout decorations were hung above the blackboards—and the boards were always black back then—and over the doors. Everything added to our holiday spirit.

Vintage postcard, House of White Birches nostalgia archives

We brought our gifts for the gift exchange on the last day. The day we got out for the holidays, we also gathered together toward the end of the day to sing carols to the accompaniment of our school's organ (which many of the teachers and some of the older students played), and we all but raised the roof in spirited song.

We also presented our Christmas program. We all did our very best, and some parents came for this entertainment.

At home, the festivities of the season lasted the entire time that we were out of school. There was visiting, and there were parties—little entertainments in the homes that included indoor games and contests, and at the end, the serving of refreshments, which was the signal that it was time to go home. Everyone tried to outdo the others with the refreshments; the tasty treats were often more important than the party itself.

Older boys and their fathers devoted a great deal of the time to hunting. Often, many of them met up and then went hunting as a group for quail, doves, rabbits and squirrels. It was a bit late in the season for hunting opossums, raccoons and other nocturnal game. Still, our dogs really got a good workout during the week of the Christmas holiday.

Serenading our neighbors was an important part of the season's activities. Groups would dress to disguise their identities, then go and sit, often without ever saying a word to reveal their identity. This was called the silent treatment, and it was lots of fun, even though it sounds far-fetched in these more sophisticated times.

One year a group went out visiting in an open-body truck, and they stopped and visited around the entire community. Some years later, some of the same people went out on a school bus. We did not visit inside the homes for the most part, but just rode around in the community—and we made lots of noise. We were a loud, talkative group, but we had so much good, clean fun.

On these trips, there were firecrackers and other fireworks. Christmas was the time for these in our neck of the woods. We celebrated the Fourth of July by going swimming and

eating the first watermelons of the season; we never associated fireworks with any time other than Christmas.

Most of us didn't have much money for Christmas spending, but we always managed to lay in supplies of fireworks. The most important were the firecrackers, shot off not so much to make a striking display of light and smoke, but to make noise. These were available in all sizes, some so large and powerful that they were downright dangerous unless special care was taken.

Roman candles—straight, cylindrical fireworks that discharged balls of fire—were also popular. Some had seven shots; the more expensive, powerful ones had as many as two dozen. These made a most striking and colorful display and ever so much loud noise. It really made for a picturesque show for us, way out on a high hill, miles from nowhere. Our fireworks could be seen from a considerable distance—and they could be heard from even farther away.

We never associated fireworks with any time other than Christmas.

Sparklers were often used. They gave off an array of sparks not unlike a shower of tiny stars. As they were harmless, some children were limited to these fireworks.

Such fireworks were available at most crossroad stores. At one time there were nine such emporia within a 5-mile radius of my home; even so, they never had a sufficient supply of fireworks to last the week. *Everybody* bought fireworks; they were such an important part of the joyous Christmas celebration as we observed it in our little world in northern Randolph County.

Few of these activities have survived the times. Certainly the fireworks—at least as we used them—are no more for the most part. It is against the law to shoot them, and I suppose it is just as well, as they are dangerous. I guess we were lucky that there never was an accident in our group.

Thinking back—and I am thinking back a few years—I remember a way of life that has pretty much disappeared and taken so much with it. Still, I have many pleasant memories of those times. ❖

Measles at Christmas, 1935

By Jacquie Weidemeyer

"Ma-a-a-ma!" Jean screeched from her bedroom. "Mama, I'm sick!"

Mama hurried to her youngest daughter. "Lewis, carry Jean into the sleeping porch where it's warm. She is running a fever and has broken out with measles."

There was an epidemic of measles running rampant in our little town of Madisonville, Texas. It had attacked our house only four days before Christmas. A rare Norther had turned our usually mild Texas December into a strange world of piercing wind. Houses in Madisonville were not built for cold weather. My room was icy—our house was never heated at night, and only the kitchen and sleeping porch were heated during the day.

My throat was scratchy, and I tried to stop a cough. I couldn't have measles and miss school. I had never in my six and a half years been tardy or absent. I had six certificates in my scrapbook to prove it. If Jean made a big enough fuss about how sick she felt, maybe I could eat my breakfast and get to the car without Mama noticing me. I dragged my shivering body out of bed and dressed as neatly as my cold hands would allow.

> *My throat was scratchy, and I tried to stop a cough. I couldn't have measles.*

But luck was on Christmas break. As I sat down for breakfast, Mama gave me a scathing look and put her hand to my brow. "You are feverish. Into the bed with Jean. You put it over on me when you had chicken pox, but not this time."

The year before, I had found five pox eruptions on my neck the Wednesday before Thanksgiving Day. I had fastened my blouse closely around my neck and gone on to school. Almost the whole of the student body had the chicken pox, so I reasoned the germs were already in the air. Mine couldn't do any more damage.

When I got home that afternoon, I "discovered" the sores. But Mama wasn't fooled. "So *that* is why your blouse was pinned so tightly around your neck." I was well by Monday morning, and did not miss a single day of school.

"I don't have splotches, so it can't be measles, and I don't have much fever."

Facing page: *Waiting Patiently for Christmas* by John Slobodnik, © House of White Birches nostalgia archives

"The fever comes before the splotches."

"Mama, I have to go to school! I can't ruin my perfect record!"

Mama never raised her voice, but she knew how to be firm. "In the bed—now."

"But I'm already dressed for school! My sole claim to fame is my perfect attendance. You've always been proud of my record."

"Lewis, please see that Jacquie gets in bed."

And that was that. I crawled into the second bed on the sleeping porch, still grumbling. "But there are only two more school days before the holidays! I could go those two days and *then* go to bed."

Mama was adamant. "You girls aren't to get out of bed."

"But we have to decorate the Christmas tree!"

"Your Aunt Ruth didn't stay in bed and be quiet and still when she had the measles. Now her eyes are crossed."

We thought about Aunt Ruth's eyes. She had had surgery twice, and still one eye was crossed. We really didn't want crossed eyes.

Jean was happy to lie still and quiet, but I fumed. We were trapped in bed for Christmas. Christmas meant relatives, and gifts wrapped in white tissue paper and tied with red and green bows. Christmas meant going to the woods and cutting down a cedar tree, and hanging our stockings from the fireplace mantel.

Mama pulled all the window shades to the bottom and closed the drapes. "I'll keep the room dark so the light won't hurt your eyes."

"You look like a Christmas quilt, Jean," I said. "You have splotches of red everywhere you don't have freckles. Just look at yourself in the mirror."

"No, I *don't* look like any quilt, and I'm not going to look at myself, so just leave me alone." Jean turned away from me toward the wall. "Mama, Jacquie's bothering me!"

There was a knock on the door of the porch. "Anyone home?" called Uncle Carlton.

Mama went to the door. "We are here, but the girls have measles."

Jacquie and Jean Gibbs.

"Then I won't come in, but here are gifts. The girls might enjoy having something to open."

We opened the packages and found handkerchief boxes. They each had a pretty picture on the top with a mirror on the inside of the lid. "Now we can see what we look like," I said. "There are no splotches on my face. Now I can go to school, and I won't be absent, just tardy."

"I'm not opening my box," Jean said. "I don't want to see myself looking terrible!"

So I kept trying to aim my mirror so that Jean would inadvertently see herself. Jean just turned her back to me. But occasionally she forgot and turned over, and then she would whine, "Mama, Jacquie is pestering me again!"

Mama quieted Jean by getting out a book. "I'll read to you from our Elsie Dinsmore book." We loved Elsie, an orphan adopted by a mean stepmother. Every kind of bad thing happened to Elsie. At least once on each page there appeared the words "And she wept." Every time Elsie wept, Mother, Jean and I cried big tears.

Mother opened the volume to the marked page. Daddy came through the room, saw what book Mama had in her hand and said, "And she wept." We laughed so that Mama couldn't read, so she made us a glass of Ovaltine.

The next morning, the first thing I saw in my handkerchief box mirror were splotches. Midmorning, Daddy came by and brought good news. "Jacquie, the school board has decided to turn out school for the holidays early. This week will not count in the attendance records. Too many students have measles. Your attendance record is still perfect."

Jean was so surprised that she turned over in bed and saw herself in the mirror. "Mama, Jacquie did it again!" She cried because I had caused her to see herself, but I was happy. I could enjoy Christmas. Being sick wasn't so bad if my perfect-attendance record was safe. ❖

A Visit From St. Nicholas

By Clement Clarke Moore

'Twas the night before Christmas,
    when all through the house
Not a creature was stirring,
    not even a mouse.
The stockings were hung
    by the chimney with care,
In hopes that St Nicholas
    soon would be there.

The children were nestled
    all snug in their beds,
While visions of sugar-plums
    danced in their heads.
And mamma in her 'kerchief,
    and I in my cap,
Had just settled our brains
    for a long winter's nap.

And then, in a twinkling,
    I heard on the roof
The prancing and pawing
    of each little hoof.
As I drew in my head,
    and was turning around,
Down the chimney St. Nicholas
    came with a bound.

He was dressed all in fur,
    from his head to his foot,
And his clothes were all tarnished
    with ashes and soot.
A bundle of Toys
    he had flung on his back,
And he looked like a peddler,
    just opening his pack.

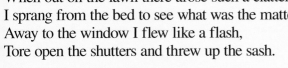

When out on the lawn there arose such a clatter,
I sprang from the bed to see what was the matter.
Away to the window I flew like a flash,
Tore open the shutters and threw up the sash.

The moon on the breast of the new-fallen snow
Gave the lustre of mid-day to objects below.
When, what to my wondering eyes should appear,
But a miniature sleigh, and eight tiny reindeer.

With a little old driver, so lively and quick,
I knew in a moment it must be St Nick.
More rapid than eagles his coursers they came,
And he whistled, and shouted,
    and called them by name!

"Now, Dasher! now, Dancer! Now, Prancer and Vixen!
On, Comet! On, Cupid! On, Donner and Blitzen!
To the top of the porch! To the top of the wall!
Now dash away! Dash away! Dash away all!"

As dry leaves that before the wild hurricane fly,
When they meet with an obstacle, mount to the sky.
So up to the house-top the coursers they flew,
With the sleigh full of Toys, and St. Nicholas too.

His eyes—how they twinkled! his dimples how merry!
His cheeks were like roses, his nose like a cherry!
His droll little mouth was drawn up like a bow,
And the beard of his chin was as white as the snow.

The stump of a pipe he held tight in his teeth,
And the smoke it encircled his head like a wreath.
He had a broad face and a little round belly,
That shook when he laughed, like a bowlful of jelly!

He was chubby and plump, a right jolly old elf,
And I laughed when I saw him, in spite of myself!
A wink of his eye and a twist of his head,
Soon gave me to know I had nothing to dread.

He spoke not a word, but went straight to his work,
And filled all the stockings, then turned with a jerk.
And laying his finger aside of his nose,
And giving a nod, up the chimney he rose!

He sprang to his sleigh, to his team gave a whistle,
And away they all flew like the down of a thistle.
But I heard him exclaim, 'ere he drove out of sight,
"Happy Christmas to all, and to all a good-night!"

Illustration from the Charles E. Graham & Co. edition of *A Visit From St. Nicholas*, 1870

Flexible Flyer

By Karl F. Welty

Winter in Dubois, in the Wind River Mountains of northwest Wyoming, always seemed incredibly long and cold. Gale-force winds often piled the snow in drifts 10 feet deep.

Winter was a time of constant chores, such as keeping the wood boxes full—one in the kitchen for the cookstove and one in the living room for short logs for the fireplace. The bedrooms were left unheated and were usually pretty cold. We used lots of blankets.

The river froze over, so we had to cut holes in the ice so the horses and cows could drink.

Winter was a time for mending harnesses and repairing machinery. It was also a time for visiting relatives and other families in the valley, some as far away as half a day's journey by horse and buggy or—if the snow was hard-packed—by horse-drawn sleigh.

Christmas was the high point of the winter. I vividly remember the winter of 1929. I was 6½ and felt I was no longer a child. I thought I should be treated the same as my older brothers and have all the things they had.

Christmas vacation was a time for sledding, especially on the hill we called Appleman's Bluff. To a child, it seemed high and steep. From the top, it took a breathtaking downward plunge at about a 30-degree angle for the first 300 or 400 feet. Then it gradually leveled out into a flat field, making a total run of a little over a quarter of a mile.

I deeply resented the fact that I did not have a sled of my own. I had to beg rides with my brothers or borrow someone's sled to make the trip solo. When I asked my dad for a sled, he just laughed and said, "Maybe Santa will bring you one for Christmas." But Mother, always practical, said I needed some warm winter clothing much more than I needed a sled.

I had reached that age when I did-but-didn't-really believe in Santa Claus. But I wanted a sled of my own so badly that I took no chances; I wrote a letter to Santa asking for only one thing—a sled.

In that part of Wyoming, Santa Claus always came late on Christmas Eve. That was when the grown-ups exchanged gifts and celebrated with Tom-and-Jerrys, a kind of eggnog laced with rum or brandy. By about 10 p.m., the gifts had all been exchanged, and I was brokenhearted. I had gotten a new sweater, rabbit-fur–lined gloves and a flashlight, but no sled. I was glumly poking at coals in the fireplace when someone said, "I hear sleigh bells."

> *I deeply resented the fact that I did not have a sled of my own.*

I rushed to the window, and sure enough, I could hear bells—and they were getting closer. Then came a knock at the door. Mother opened it, and in came Santa with a loud "Ho, ho, ho!" Then he asked, "Where is Karl Jr.?"

"Here! Here!" I shouted. Santa was carrying the most magnificent sled I had ever seen. It had bright red runners and a varnished wooden top. "Flexible Flyer" was printed on it in red letters outlined with black, and it had a braided rope to pull it with.

Santa picked me up, gave me a hug and said, "I got your letter, and I made a special trip to bring you a very special sled." Then, with a wave and a shout of "Merry Christmas to all!" he jumped back into the sleigh and sped off.

I remember wondering, *Why was Santa's sleigh pulled by Dad's old horse, Frank, instead of reindeer?*

That was a Christmas I will never forget. ❖

Facing page: *Sledding With Grandpa* by Alan Foster © 1930 SEPS: Licensed by Curtis Publishing

MERRY XMAS

The Night Santa Dropped In

By Stan Johnson

When I think of Christmas, my mind takes me back to Christmas Eve 1931, when my brother was 4 and I was almost 7. We lived on a farm some 12 miles from Mitchell, S.D. It was the start of the Depression, and money was hard to come by. It looked to my brother and me like we might have a very slim Christmas. Our mother had told us we might have to settle for a couple pair of socks or mittens. We were pretty well prepared for that, and we were pretty sure that Santa Claus probably wouldn't be stopping this far out in the country.

We had eaten supper, and our father put on his heavy coat and overshoes, and said he was going to give the cows another feed of hay. This was the way he usually did things when it was too cold for the cows to be out of the barn. Often I would go along with him, but that Christmas Eve, he said I didn't have to help. So my brother and I just rolled around on the floor in front of the old heater.

After a little while, our father came into the house again and asked, "Did you hear something while I was out in the barn?"

"No!" we replied. "We didn't hear anything. Why?"

> *We were pretty sure that Santa probably wouldn't be stopping this far out in the country.*

Then he said, "While I was out in the barn, I thought I heard bells. That had to be Santa! Where else did *this* come from?" Then he dragged a good-size box into the living room.

The box contained several smaller boxes, and my brother and I began to open them. In one box there was a little International tractor. In the next was an International threshing machine; then came a team of horses and a little wagon with a grain box on it. Wow, were we excited!

We made belts out of rubber bands and played we were threshing grain. Some time after Christmas, our father helped us make a little hayrack to fit the little wagon.

The only complaint associated with those wonderful gifts was that Mother didn't like us running the tractor across the linoleum floors because the lugs on the tractor wheels made a lot of noise.

We played with our little threshing set for years—long after we had realized who Santa Claus really was. If only I still had that set so that I could pass it on to some of our great-grandchildren.

It didn't take a whole lot to give us a merry Christmas in those days. ❖

A Basket Full Of Christmas

By Rae Cross

Today as I browsed through a Goodwill store, I saw a big wicker clothes basket. Memories of Christmas past rushed in. I didn't realize how long I had stared at the basket until a clerk asked if she might help. When I said, "No, thank you, I was just thinking about Christmas," she gave me an odd look, and I felt certain, passed the word I should be watched. Thinking about it later, I can understand her concern because Christmas and clothes baskets don't seem to have much in common. However, at our house, years ago, the two were almost synonymous.

Immediately after Thanksgiving dinner, we all began urging Mother, "Now can we put the basket out?" Reluctantly, she always agreed—reluctantly because the only place it could be placed was on top of the huge grand piano that dominated the living room with its bulk. That piano was Mother's prized possession, and nothing, but *nothing*, was placed on its polished top until it was carefully padded and protected from scratch and stain.

Christmas and clothes baskets don't seem to have much in common.

Finally pronounced ready, the oversize basket with red bows tied on each handle was placed on top of the blankets and coverings, and Christmas began.

Even if we could have afforded a tree, the room could not have accommodated both the tree and the piano. Certainly a tree could not have brought more happiness or excitement than the clothes basket did. As days passed, packages were placed in it, and our suspense increased.

We knew most presents would, of necessity, be useful: clothes, mittens, boots, caps, earmuffs, scarves. Knowing that did not dampen our impatience or anticipation, however, for each family member also received "fun gifts." These gifts were to cost no more than 10 cents, but it was amazing what you could buy at the dime store in those days—and oh, the thrill of shopping!

These little gifts were wrapped so no one could guess what the packages contained. There were little packages, big packages and middle-sized packages, all wrapped in tissue paper and decorated with pictures cut from magazines and papers.

When at last the wonderful day finally came, and my father lifted the overflowing basket onto the floor, we all gathered 'round. Since I was youngest, I generally was privileged to call out the names and deliver the gifts.

We never knew whether a package would contain a warm sweater, long johns or one of the fun items, such as a pencil (maybe an advertising one from a local store, but so what—it would write), shoehorn, thimble, jackknife, shoestrings, tape measure, eraser, package of needles, handkerchief, hair ribbons, buttonhook, dust cap, pocket comb, candy bar, jacks or whistle. Each gift brought shouts of joy and unaffected pleasure.

When the bottom of the basket was reached, Mother always said, "Now we can put all the dirty clothes in the basket and clear off the top of the piano."

Somehow we knew that meant she wanted to be asked to play the Christmas hymns we knew so well. Never did a happier group gather around and sing with all the ardor of the true Christmas spirit and our family relationship.

The empty basket at the Goodwill store was reminiscent of the emptiness I know now at this season when it is no longer possible to enjoy the love and companionship of those happy days.

And yet, I envision the Christmas basket full and running over with gratitude for the love and blessings the years have brought so generously to me and mine.

And now I hope that everyone everywhere may have a Christmas basket—real and mental—full of life's necessities along with enough fun to lighten life's seriousness, and always a song to summarize the meaning and the glory of the day. ❖

Grandma's Lasting Gift

By Helen Oyakawa

Baban, my father's mother, didn't believe in buying anything unless it was absolutely, utterly necessary. I learned this as a young girl in the late 1930s when I spent one week every year with her and *Jichan*, my grandfather, in Hawaii. She felt that table salt was just as good as store-bought Colgate or Pepsodent for brushing teeth. It made my mouth tingle, but I didn't complain.

She believed in the daily bath, but she didn't leave a bar of soap around for me to waste. She rubbed it into my washcloth. I always ran out of suds before I was halfway through scrubbing myself, but I didn't grumble.

She cracked two fresh eggs in a bowl over hot, steaming rice. Along with her version of "sunny side up," she served a jar of home-made pickles and a large plate of vegetables from her garden. What a delicious meal! And there was that one time when she gave me a nickel to buy ice cake at the store down the hill, I was so grateful that I couldn't ask for anything more.

"You look like a Christmas tree," my brothers teased.

She didn't have a single toy for me to play with, but I didn't ask for one. Baban expected me to entertain myself. My grandparents didn't own a radio, but they had something better—a phonograph, which I taught myself to crank to produce music. I joyfully sang and danced to the lively Japanese songs while my grandparents watched and smiled.

They lived at the top of a column of identical wooden duplex houses that had been built for plantation workers. Each family unit had two bedrooms, a breezeway and a kitchen. Several feet beyond that, they shared another small, covered duplex with their own laundry sink and an outdoor toilet with a constant stream of water running below. People bathed at one of the community baths, which were segregated for men and women.

I loved standing in the middle of Baban and Jichan's house, feeling the air drift through all the breezeways from the Pacific Ocean to the tip of the hill behind us.

Jichan and Baban were white-haired, peaceful and slightly bent. They didn't talk much, but they listened to me even though they didn't understand my excited flow of pidgin English. Best of all, they never scolded. They read the newspapers and puttered around their place.

I loved walking along other families' private gardens, and I wondered why my grandparents grew only vegetables. When I asked them why *they* didn't grow beautiful periwinkles, golden asters, red carnations and white gladioli, they replied, "You can't eat flowers." I didn't argue.

I was too busy creating dishes, and pots and pans out of mud. I constructed dams and swimming pools for make-believe elves and fairies. I peered into the slanting wooden flume, hoping to see and hear the stalks of sugar cane go whooshing downhill to the mill by the sea.

I made daily excursions to check on the huge chicken house. I was thrilled and intimidated by the incessant clucking of the hundreds of hens that my grandparents' neighbors raised to sell thousands of eggs.

One day I picked a bunch of black seeds growing on spinach vines and crushed some. That's how I invented paint. Using chopsticks and an old brush, I sketched my world and wrote words on scraps of butcher paper and newsprint that Baban had stacked aside neatly to reuse. When I showed my creations to them, they rewarded me with astonishment and praise.

When she came to visit my family in Kona one holiday, Baban handed me a small brown bag. I thanked her, hardly expecting to find anything inside that I secretly wished for.

Was I wrong! Wonder of wonders, she had read my mind. I found a black velvet headband with saucy crimson bows at the ends, an artificial pink rose corsage, and a long necklace shimmering with glass beads in a rainbow of colors. And as if that weren't enough, I saw not just one but *two* cards of bobby pins.

I was so happy that I cried, and I blubbered "Thank you!" a hundred times. How had she known that I had ached for gifts such as these? Without hesitation, I put them on, all at the same time.

My mother and father laughed. "You look like a Christmas tree," my brothers teased. But I took their words as a compliment. I felt like I was the luckiest child in the world.

Even today, when I think back to that time, I know I didn't receive *things*. My dear Baban gave me a rich, glowing, lasting Christmas memory—a huge, generous gift—that will shine forever in my heart. ❖

Christmas Bells

By Henry Wadsworth Longfellow

I heard the bells on Christmas Day
Their old, familiar carols play,
And wild and sweet
The words repeat
Of peace on earth, good-will to men!
And thought how, as the day had come,
The belfries of all Christendom

Had rolled along
The unbroken song
Of peace on earth, good-will to men!
Till, ringing, singing on its way
The world revolved from night to day,

A voice, a chime,
A chant sublime
Of peace on earth, good-will to men!
Then from each black, accursed mouth
The cannon thundered in the South,

And with the sound
The Carols drowned
Of peace on earth, good-will to men!
It was as if an earthquake rent
The hearth-stones of a continent,

And made forlorn
The households born
Of Peace on earth, good-willl to men!
And in despair I bowed my head;
'There is no peace on earth,' I said;

'For hate is strong,
And mocks the song
Of peace on earth, good-will to men!'
Then pealed the bells more loud and deep:
'God is not dead; nor doth he sleep!

The Wrong shall fail,
The Right prevail,
With peace on earth, good-will to men!'

Holiday Remembrance

By Florence J. Paul

*I*t was December, the month in which we commemorate two festivals of lights. First came the Jewish Hanukkah, which precedes Christmas by 200 years and is a reminder of the first war fought for freedom of conscience and religion. When I was 7 years old, we lived in a small town partially surrounded by cemeteries. Visitors would shudder and wonder how we could live so close to cemeteries. At the time, I was too young to understand the significance. I didn't understand why anyone was repelled by the fact that our house faced the graveyard. In later years, we would laugh and say, "The dead are certainly more harmless than the living."

On one side of the cemetery our house faced stood an inn that had a sign over the entrance announcing that it was the meeting place of survivors of the *General Slocum,* a ferry that had been in an accident that took the lives of many passengers. The pealing bells in the church that stood in that cemetery were the most beautiful I have ever heard.

Hanukkah passed very quietly for us, as there was not enough money for necessities let alone a menorah, candles and gifts. My Jewish friends showed off their little gifts, but none of my four brothers or I ever discussed it at home. Instinctively we knew that if our wonderful mom had been able to, we also would have had a festive holiday. But she always repeated the fascinating story of the Maccabees to us.

Following the eight days of Hanukkah was Christmas. Local shops were decorated and ringed with colored lights. I loved walking along at night—back when people were still able to walk the streets at night—and seeing the colored lights reflected on the fresh white snow. To me it was a fairyland.

Our little town had no Santa Clauses ringing bells on the street corners, but my Christian friends all had trees in their homes with delicate colored balls hanging all over them. Some even had shining silver stars on top. At the bases were beautifully wrapped boxes awaiting Christmas Eve.

I was awed by all that magnificence and the mysterious gifts in the boxes. What I didn't realize at the time was that the gifts in the boxes were practical items; while most of our neighbors were better off financially than my family, they were not wealthy enough to splurge on fulfilling the children's dreams. Most of the packages contained mittens, gloves, galoshes, ties, underwear and so on.

On Christmas Day, they all had ham or turkey dinners to which I would occasionally be invited. My invitations were only to turkey dinners, as my friends knew that people of the Jewish faith did not eat pork. They didn't know why— nor did I at that time—but they respected it.

One day when my ball went over the fence and into the cemetery, I climbed through the opening made by years of children pushing through to retrieve a ball or play hide-and-seek. Many of the tombstones were decorated for Christmas with wreaths, pine branches with red poinsettia leaves tucked in and flowers. Lying on the ground near my ball was a single pine branch, about 12 inches long, with several shoots covered with pine needles. I took a needle off, rubbed it between my fingers and put it to my nose. The heavenly scent of fresh pine was delightful. I picked up my ball and left, holding the pine branch.

On the walk home, as luck would have it, I spotted a small cardboard box, slightly soiled but in fine shape otherwise. An idea came to me, and I took the box home with me also.

My mother wasn't home, so I went to my bedroom, which I shared with my younger brother. I made a pencil hole in the center of the box, placed it on my chair and stuck the end of the branch into the hole.

Then I sat on my bed and thought about how to decorate it. After a short while, it came to me.

I made tiny balls of cotton. Then I dipped some in blue ink and some in red ink that my oldest brother had on his desk, and left some of them white. I laid the wet ones to dry on the waxed paper in which the butter had been wrapped. In the meantime, rummaging through a small junk drawer, I found the glass vial I was looking for, which contained tiny glass beads.

With needle and thread, I made several strings with four beads on each, leaving enough extra string to tie each onto a branch. When the cotton balls were dry enough, I strung thread through them and hung them on branches, alternating them with the beaded strings. Then I admired my handiwork. To me, it was beautiful.

In the drawer, I was thrilled to find more beads. I threaded them carefully in a double strand, then wrapped them in a paper napkin and tied it with a ribbon I had been saving. Then I wrote "Mom" on the napkin and placed it at the base of my "tree."

I pointed to the gift. "Mom, it's really a Hanukkah gift, but it looks pretty under the tree."

When my mother came home, I took her hand and led her into my bedroom and over to the tree. She stared quietly at it. I pointed to the gift. "Mom, it's really a Hanukkah gift, but it looks pretty under the tree."

I noticed a tear in her eyes. She opened the package, held up the necklace and said, "How lovely" as she put it on. Then she sat on my bed, put her arms around me and held me close. I loved the clean smell of her and would have enjoyed staying so, but she soon held me away a little so she could look into my eyes.

"My darling," she said, her voice a little husky, "thank you so much. I will always keep and enjoy this lovely necklace. From today on, we will save our pennies so that next year, we'll have a real Hanukkah celebration."

I did not know until years later that she arranged to do work for a nearby family one day a week while we were in school to supplement my dad's Depression-era salary. She took my brother along, and he played with the family's child while she worked. Each week, she put $2 into a Christmas Club account at our local bank.

Nothing could have dimmed the satisfaction I received from her pleasure, even when my brother said, "Boy, what a dumb thing that is."

Her happiness was a holiday gift to me that I will treasure forever. ❖

A Howling Success

By Helen Wanamaker Vail

I'm sitting here at my dining room table, sipping a cup of freshly brewed coffee and taste-testing my new Snow-Covered Raspberry Blossom Cookies. Since it's only a few days till Christmas, and most of my wrapping, cookie making and menus are planned, I have a few minutes to let my mind race ahead to New Year's Eve. I'm remembering how we used to ring in the new year when we were kids.

That was the one night when we were allowed to stay up past 8 o'clock. Daddy, Mother and Grandpop Wanamaker would sit around the old Zenith radio, staying toasty warm from the coal stove in the corner of the living room while they waited for Guy Lombardo to start the countdown to the new year.

We kids, all half-asleep on the carpet, waited for our parents to shake us awake. About five minutes before midnight, Mother would gently rouse us so we could don our warm coats, mittens and hats. Then we grabbed her well-worn pots, pans, lids and wooden spoons—metal spoons if we wanted to make more noise.

And this kid did!

We then stepped out into the night air that was so cold it took our breath away. How exciting! I still remember shivering, not only from the cold air but also from the excitement of what was about to happen.

All of a sudden, Grandpop yelled, "Start making your racket, kiddies!" What a laugh that was! You can bet that that healthy bunch of kids really made some noise.

Our neighbors in our small, rural area were enjoying the celebration also. We could hear them laughing, tooting horns and banging on pots and pans. Some were even setting off firecrackers.

But my dog, Tiny, hated all the racket. He would start howling, and before long, dogs within miles were howling along with him. But wait a minute—how could we be sure that the noise was hurting their ears? Could it be that this was their way of saying "Happy New Year!" to each other?

After we finished our noisemaking, we hurried back inside to steaming mugs of hot tea and to make our New Year's resolutions.

I never kept mine!

The next afternoon, we had our customary roast pork, sauerkraut, creamy mashed potatoes and homemade applesauce, perhaps with mince pie or spicy applesauce cake for dessert. All in all, it was a fitting final farewell to the holiday and a fresh beginning for a sparkling, happy, healthy new year. ❖

Guy Lombardo, House of White Birches nostalgia archives

A New Year's Celebration

By Dorothy Weaver

Holidays in our home were very important for us. I had nine brothers and sisters, so you can imagine there was a houseful. Seven of us grew to adulthood, so with the regular holidays and all of our birthdays, there was always a celebration of some kind going on.

Outside of Christmas, the one celebration that was special to me was New Year's Eve. It was a time for making resolutions that were usually broken the next day. One of my parents' resolutions was that we'd all be together as a family on New Year's Eve to usher in the new year.

My older sister had given my dad a double-barrel shotgun a long time ago. I was a very little girl then, as I was on the tail end of the family and my sister was the oldest.

But I remember my dad cleaning and polishing his gun. There wasn't a speck of dust or dirt on it. He liked to go pheasant hunting around our home in Omaha, Neb. That gun was part of him, and he took excellent care of it.

Several days before New Year's Eve, preparations for the holiday would begin. Dad would start polishing and cleaning his gun, and Mother would make plans for our meal together. She would make oyster stew and let it simmer

I BRING YOU A HAPPY NEW YEAR

Vintage postcard, House of White Birches nostalgia archives

all day; that was our traditional feast. There were also beef dishes, because several of us—including me—didn't like seafood. There were desserts of several kinds too.

Around 10 p.m., the family started gathering, and after prayer, we all enjoyed Mother's feast. As midnight approached, we all went outside into the bitter cold. There was nearly always snow on the ground. My dad put the shells in his gun, and as 12 o'clock struck, he would shoot both barrels into the air with a deafening blast.

We brought in the new year with new hopes and dreams for everyone.

There was a lot of yelling and clapping; it was a joyous time for all. Some of our neighbors joined us in the celebration.

As we got older, married and had families of our own, we were still expected to come to our parents' house for New Year's Eve. Some of us attended other parties, too, but we left in time to come home for oyster stew and ringing in the new year together. We brought our friends along too.

My parents and most of my brothers and sisters have passed on now, but there is never a New Year's Eve that I don't relive those precious memories again.

I can still see my father, standing with his gun pointed to the sky, and saying, "Happy New Year, everybody!" ❖

Happy New Year!

By Laura Steele

"Start the New Year out right!" my dad said jovially each Dec. 31. Resolutions were solemnly sworn—to study harder; to get some A's on the report card; to quit teasing sister so much; and when we were older, to find a job in the midst of the Depression; to lose weight; and to visit old Aunt Susie more often.

In the 1920s, my folks had neighbors in to play cards while we children, who were held to our strict 8 p.m. bedtime, retired. But at the witching hour of midnight, we were awakened to run outside in our nightgowns, and bang and rattle spoons against pie tins while we yelled lustily into the black night: "Happy New Year!"

Echoes reverberated from house to house—"Happy New Year!" Firecrackers sputtered. A toy cannon boomed. Our neighbor's gun ripped the night air with a deafening sound, and answering gunshots crackled from hill to hill, becoming fainter in the distance. Then, after two or three minutes, the clattering night became silent once more.

Echoes reverberated from house to house—"Happy New Year!"

Back into the house we slipped, shivering with cold and excitement, ready for that warm glass of milk and cookies for the wee ones, and something stronger for the adults. We crept into bed with a feeling of satisfaction. The past was dead. Better times were a-coming—that is, if we were strong enough to keep those resolutions.

As we grew into our teens, we were allowed to have New Year parties with our friends. We played cards, with prizes from the 10-cent store; we danced with the rug rolled up in the corner, or we sang popular songs around the piano until the midnight dash for the door to honk horns, crank noisemakers and yell.

However late parties might last, everyone was up at dawn on New Year's Day. Relatives came from all directions, for ours was their halfway house to the Pasadena Rose Parade. Rather than fight the traffic and try vainly to find parking space, they all gathered at our home and walked in the crisp morning air over the hill and across the Arroyo Seco Bridge to the parade of fantasyland floats and prancing horses.

Anyone who has seen the Rose Parade knows what a beautiful beginning to the New Year it is, combining the artistry of designers and the work of hundreds who press rainbows of flowers into the animated creations. Tucked amidst pink and yellow, red and mauve petals, the lucky queen and her ladies shiver in the cold air, but keep a constant smile as they wave to the shouting crowd. The best of Arabians, pintos, and honey-colored palominos dressed in polished silver glint in the sun as they prance. Bands from many states beat out stirring music, while majorettes high-step, flinging twirling batons high in the air.

The sights and sounds of the Rose Parade have been part of our New Year's celebrations since 1922 with the exception of the World War II years. Each year, we trudged home from the parade, tired from standing in the crowds, but anticipating a scrumptious noonday feast. Potluck brought by each family was spread out on the buffet. A turkey and ham took the center, joined by huge bowls of potato salad, baked beans, green salads, Jell-O, fruits and hot casseroles (usually of a Mexican style, a Southern Californian specialty).

Piling a plate high with the goodies, each person searched for a comfortable spot in a chair or sprawled on the floor to listen to the Rose Bowl football game amidst friendly cheering and booing for different sides.

After the game, dessert appeared on the sideboard. Samples of apple and pumpkin pies, chocolate and angel food cakes, cookies and homemade candies were carefully chosen.

Now it was time to divulge all the New Year resolutions, and to take the kidding and laughs if you had failed to live up to last year's prescribed aims. Predictions of upcoming marriages, new jobs and so forth were written down to be read the following year.

At this time, too, Mother's cousin Johnny passed out diaries to everyone of teen age and younger, urging them to note happenings throughout the year. Johnny could be counted on to provide the right dates for births, deaths, marriages, blizzards, floods and such, and he claimed it was because of the diaries he had kept since childhood.

But tragedy struck when Johnny was but 40 years old. Coming in from work, he turned on the gas heater and lay down for a nap. In those days, gas heaters were deadly if one forgot to open a window. His body was found three days later.

Johnny was sadly missed at our next New Year's observance. Still, his teachings about the importance of family history prompted us to keep records for generations to come.

For many years our New Year's customs have followed the same pattern. Television, however, now lures some of the family to watch the Rose Parade at home; only the more agile make the hike over the hill. Tape recordings of resolutions take the place of written ones. The older folks have long since passed away, and we who were children in 1922 are now great-grandparents. But we have seen many happy New Year's Days. ❖

Rose Parade 1949

By Jerilyn Stone Lupu

The showroom at Uptown Chevrolet on Colorado Boulevard in Pasadena, Calif., was cleared. It was another New Year's Day, and Papa (my grandfather) had taken the shiny new automobiles out of his showroom and had erected bleachers to give members of his "Uptown family," as he called his employees and their children, choice seats for the Rose Parade.

Papa participated in the Rose Parade every year from the mid-1930s through the 1950s. Papa always rode on horseback with the Los Angeles Sheriff's Posse, on Silver Joy, his champion Tennessee walking horse. Silver Joy's white colts, Thunder and Lightning, carried the buglers heralding the parade.

The 1949 Rose Parade was special because my family and I rode on Papa's Uptown Chevrolet float. We had gone to Hollywood to rent costumes of 1899 vintage from a movie costume supplier.

My heavily embroidered gray wool coat had a collar as big as a saucer. Daddy sported a tweed suit, bowler hat and mustache.

The back lot at Uptown was used for body work on damaged cars. This was where the Uptown family, including my parents, two sisters and I, gathered the day before New Year's, among glue pots and baskets of flowers, to paste blossoms through the chicken-wire frame covering the wooden skeleton and the car underneath.

Though I longed to fasten the bright orange bird-of-paradise plants, we children were allowed to glue only the gold and white chrysanthemums. I carefully brushed the underside of each mum with glue and pressed it through a diamond-shaped opening in the wire.

Papa furnished box lunches for all. When our tummies were full and our bodies warm from the sunshine, we could barely contain our excitement, anticipating our hour of fame along with the beautiful Rose Queen and her princesses.

On parade day we were up before dawn, ready to be outfitted and seated in the beautifully decorated surrey.

"Going to Sunday School" was Uptown Chevrolet's float in the 1949 Rose Parade.

The parade passed slowly. Bands stopped at intervals and entertained the crowd as drum majors and baton twirlers performed. Monty Montana twirled a lariat. An ice skater performed on a pool of ice surrounded by flowers.

After three hours, Mother and Daddy's laps were soaked, the toddlers were wailing, and we were thirsty and needed a bathroom. At the end, however, we had to remain in our places until the judges had viewed our float.

Many years have passed. Uptown, Papa, and Silver Joy are gone. But I'll never forget watching them entertain audiences in the shadow of Mount Baldy in the warm, fragrant California sunshine. ❖

The Best Valentine

By Rita Larkin Kayse

"Are you sure the kids will like these valentines?" I asked for the 10th time.

"Yes, dear," Mama answered patiently, adding a tiny bow to the kitten I had pasted to a heart. "These cards are what valentines are meant to be, real expressions of your feelings for someone. How could your friends *not* like them?"

I sure hoped Mama was right. Tomorrow would be Valentine's Day 1953, and all the kids at school would exchange cards. Mama had said we couldn't afford to buy cards that year, so we'd make some instead. The cotton crop had failed on our little southeast Missouri farm the year before, and Daddy had had to go to Oregon to find work in the lumber camps.

Mama knew how important Valentine's Day was to me, so she had saved old greeting cards, bits of ribbon and lace, old seed catalogs and every brightly colored advertisement she could get.

My brothers, ages 11 and 12, had decided they were too grown-up for valentines, but they watched with interest as the jumbled mess on the dining table soon turned into a stack of clever valentines. Each card was custom-made for my friends in third grade.

"I'm going to get the best valentine of all," Mama said shyly as we cleared the table and stacked our creations.

"You're getting a valentine?" scoffed Dennis. "Grown-ups don't get valentines!"

"Is Daddy going to send you one from Oregon?" I asked.

"No," said Mama, biting her lip. "Now run along to bed, all of you."

"That was a dumb question," ridiculed Don as we walked to our rooms. "Mama and Daddy are old. Why would he send her a valentine?"

Mama and Daddy were in their 50s, so I had to agree they did seem awfully old for love and all that mushy stuff.

The next morning, we raced to the breakfast table full of questions. "Where's your valentine? Did you get your valentine?"

Mama wore a secret smile as she dished out oatmeal. "No, but the day's not over yet. Now hush and eat, or you'll be late for school."

The almost-2-mile walk to school took a long time, and today of all days, I didn't want to be late, so I ate quickly. At the party, my classmates got so excited over the valentines made especially for them that once again, I realized I should never doubt Mama.

That afternoon we were walking home from school when Mama came bouncing down the rutted road in our old car. "Jump in, kids, let's go get my valentine!" she said excitedly. Bewildered, we piled into the car, full of questions. Mama just smiled and drove on down the muddy road faster than I'd ever seen her drive. Why was she acting so strange?

Mama pulled up to the grocery store that was also a feed store and bus station. "No, stay here," she said softly as we started to get out of the car with her. She had taken only a few steps before a sleek silver bus slowed to a stop in front of the station and a tall, gray-haired man stepped off.

Daddy was home from Oregon!

We watched in fascination as Mama ran to collect her valentine in her arms. That was the day my brothers and I learned that love and all that mushy stuff isn't only for the young. ❖

A Valentine From Dad

By Starrlette L. Howard

Looking back across the years on the paths of valentines, a few vivid memories come to mind. Dad worked the graveyard shift as a civil service worker at the air base, so he was coming home on the dark side of morning just as Mom and we three kids were getting up to greet the winter's day. It was not unlike Dad to gather Mom into his arms and begin to dance to the soft sounds of the radio playing in the background. Even as a child, I thought of my parents as denim and lace, and as romantic as the movie musicals.

They loved holidays of all kinds, and there would be remembrance gifts for each other and for us kids. Dad gave Mom huge, heart-shaped boxes of chocolates on Valentine's Day until she told him she was watching her weight and instead would welcome a music box. Thereafter, over the years, music boxes came to fill Mom's house.

As the winter day dawned silver and coral, we sat down to half a grapefruit with a slice of maraschino cherry on top. We kids tried to drown the pucker power by pouring salt or sugar over our citrus fruit. Cold milk oozed into our bowls of hot oatmeal, and for crispness on the menu, we'd have a piece or two of cinnamon toast. At a very early age, we learned, "Waste not, want not."

> *It was unheard of not to bring a valentine for everyone in the class.*

After breakfast, I'd slip into my coat and gather up my shoe-box valentine holder. There were always prizes for the best-decorated shoe box, but I never won, though I spent many creative and tedious hours with scissors, glue, construction paper and sometimes kitchen foil. Once I made a shoe box look like a rural mailbox, and once like a toy bus. But regardless of how much Dad and Mom raved about my boxes, they never won a prize.

Then I would gather the valentines for my classmates. My favorites as I got older came in a punch-out *Valentines and Activity Booklet*. It was fun to spend a winter evening picking out the best valentines for friends and using the rest for the "other kids." It was unheard of to not bring a valentine for everyone in the class. And of course, we fashioned our own construction-paper valentines for our parents and grandparents.

The distant sun would just be rising over the mountain as I kissed my parents and left for school. I had a full two blocks to go across some fields, and on cold days, the ice-topped snow would scrape my legs above my rubber boots. Rebelliously leaving the woolen leggings for younger kids who weren't too big to be embarrassed by them, I paid a dear price, for girls always wore dresses to school then. About half-way to school, an inner voice always told me it was as close to home as to school, but I didn't heed that voice too often.

When I got to school and opened the door, a flood of warm air enveloped me as I reached the coat rack. Holidays were really only half-days of school. After lunch we'd get to sing songs, do artwork or perhaps even see a movie like *Charlie, the Lonesome Cougar.* And homeroom mothers would bring treats like cupcakes or big, heart-shaped sugar cookies with swirls of pink or white frosting. It's hard, but almost any kid can handle half a day's schoolwork when they know that after lunch, they can break away from the monotony of the day-to-day schedule.

However, it wasn't exchanging valentines at school that was one of my favorite memories—it was returning home. For there, propped up on my bed, would be a small, red, heart-shaped box of valentine chocolates and a card signed "With love from Dad." Perhaps Mom had her lovely hand in the annual tradition as well, but in my eyes, Dad was a romantic hero.

I suppose growing up and becoming a young bride might have changed this annual sweet spot, except that Dad had a hand in that too. The first year my sister and I were married, Dad called our fellows into the garage under the guise of working on a mechanical problem. He asked the young men if either of them had a valentine for his wife. Neither did. He presented them each with a big, heart-shaped box of chocolates. "It's never too late or too early to remember the one you love," he advised. And I'm sure his warm brown eyes sparkled.

Thirty years later, the tradition continues with my husband. I still love to send valentines and receive them from friends and relatives, but I will always remember how very special a valentine from Dad made me feel. There's a warmth and joy about being loved that even cold, old winter cannot chase away. ❖

When Grandpa was a little boy, and Grandmama was little, too,
He sent a Valentine to her—just like this one I'm sending you.

Paste F, G, and H on white paper before you put the valentine together

Old-Time Valentine Pattern

Editor's Note: This pattern for a homemade valentine card (and the illustration on page 155) were printed in the February 1920 issue of *McCall's* magazine.

This reproduction is slightly smaller than the original.

From

BARBARA HALE

Cut eleven tabs of white paper like this—and fold like this→

fold back

fold tab here

fold back here

Paste one end of a folded tab on back of doves A

A

Paste one end of a folded tab on back of flowers, B.

B

Paste one end of a folded tab on back of flowers, C.

C

Slip end D of tab through slot D in heart and slip end E of tab through slot E in heart.

D   E

Paste other end of tab with doves   A

B Paste other end of tab with flowers

C Paste other end of tab with flowers

To MY VALENTINE

F

Paste F on end of tabs on G — and be sure to have hearts just over each other.

Paste end of a folded tab here

Paste end of a folded tab here

Paste end of a folded tab here

Paste end of a folded tab here

H

Paste end of a folded tab here

cut out along this line

Paste end of a folded tab here

Paste end of a folded tab here

Paste end of a folded tab here

G

Paste G on end of tabs on H

Little Chocolate Heart

By Dorothy Cole Clayton

February is a grim, cold month along the northern shore of Massachusetts, when all outdoors seems wrapped in a dark shroud. But I remember that for a welcome few days, the entrance to the Woolworth's store opened the way to a magic spot.

When I opened the door, I was greeted by a blast of steam-heated air and the spectacular sight of valentine decorations.

Red, gold, silver and white cupids hung from the light fixtures.

The candy counter had all types of sugar hearts—some printed with sayings—and shiny red cinnamon hearts for just a nickel a bag.

On our way home from school, we made a detour to Woolworth's to visit its gigantic garden of valentine delights.

The absolute *pièce de résistance* was the small counter covered with a smooth layer of white oilcloth. This was where personalized chocolate hearts were prepared in a variety of sizes.

Once a customer had picked the size, the salesgirl took the money and asked how to spell the name. Then, with all the dignity and majesty of Michelangelo, she picked up a pastry tube full of pink icing and printed the name at an angle across the chocolate heart. She never wasted a jot of icing.

I coveted one of those hearts, but did not ask for it. My sisters and I told our mother about them, but only so she could enjoy the idea of a treat.

We knew financing even a modest celebration was a challenge to her weekly budget. Her school-age children each needed a quarter to buy valentines for their friends.

Sometimes our daddy brought home red lollipops for us. As for personalized chocolate hearts, he said, "They'll just eat them, and it won't matter if their names are on them."

I was upset because Mama usually did as Daddy suggested. But to my great joy, she replied, "They'll remember it as a lovely treat, Jack."

My mother understood how much it would mean to Arlene, Mary, Eleanor and me to have a personalized chocolate heart. Rita, the baby, would not need one. Brother Billy would want one, just to eat it.

And so that year, when I was 10 years old, my mother set aside enough money to buy the least-expensive hearts for us. On the great day, I held the $2.50 because I was the oldest girl.

After school, we walked into Woolworth's and up to that counter. It was a proud moment when we told the salesgirl our names and their spellings. The young lady put the decorated hearts in white paper bags and admonished us to carry them carefully so the names would not get smudged.

Mama was right about the happy memories those special treats gave us. I can still see that little heart with my name written across it in pink. I can't summon the taste, but I do remember—and thank you, Mama. ❖